A Beachcomber's Odyssey

Volume I

Treasures from a Collected Past

by S. Deacon Ritterbush, Ph. D.

Intro photo by Celia Pearson

Editor: D.S. Russell
Creative Design: S. Deacon Ritterbush
Photo Styling: S. Deacon Ritterbush and Megan Elyse Lloyd
Production: Jill Flanagan Madsen and Megan Elyse Lloyd

Library of Congress Cataloging-in-Publication Data

First edition 2008

Published in the United States by
Ritz Dotter Publishers
P.O. Box 5939,
Annapolis, MD 21403
ritzdotter@gmail.com

ISBN: 978-0-9818705-0-2

Note: This compilation represents opinions by the author, her consultants and editors, as well as references to
historical events and geographical data provided by authors noted in footnotes or in the bibliography. Every effort
has been made to validate dates and events, however conflicting information was sometimes given. The science
sections of this book are intended to give readers a general "taste" of each region and artifact under discussion
with the hope that their appetites are sufficiently wetted so they want to conduct research on their own beach
explorations and the treasures that they find.

Printed and bound in China by Oceanic Graphic Printing, Inc.

Cover photos by Megan Elyse Lloyd

For Nancy and Ritt,
who gave me the beach,
which is always a good start.

Table of Contents

Preface
Footprints in the Sand

A red beach marble shelters under the lip of a mid-20th century milk bottle. Beside them is a lavender-shaded bottle lip from the early 1900s.

Preface: *Footprints in the Sand*

No matter what I say,
All I really love
Is the rain that flattens on the bay,
And the eel grass in the cove,
And the jingle shells that lie and bleach
At the tideline; and the trace
Of higher tides along the beach…

Edna St. Vincent Millay

I am a casual beachcomber. My goal has never been to find the most exotic shell or colorful piece of sea glass. Nor do I plan vacations around beaches famous for shells, artifacts or fossils. However, if there is a beach nearby (and during my lifetime, that has been often) I go there for a stroll at least once a week to treasure hunt. If an interesting shape or special color catches my eye, I'll pick it up and, if deemed worthy, happily stuff it into my pocket.

Nearly every beach yields at least one prize too precious not to keep, though these days I pocket less than I used to. One's house can only hold so much.

My sandy footprints have crisscrossed the globe, from gracious Chesapeake Bay to Scotland's verdant Orkney Islands; from languid Tongan islets and the colonial heat of Jamaica to the brisk, windswept shores of New England's Martha's Vineyard and Nantucket Islands. Each beach offered up natural and man-made wonders whose beauty, form or history delighted or intrigued me.

The most precious of these mementos now rest on windowsills, mantles and bookshelves throughout my home. Whenever I come upon one, memories flood in of a particular day on that particular beach. These memories open me like a book, flipping the pages of my life back to the mood and temper of those times, and I can recall the life lessons I learned while walking on that beach. Just as I have tucked these special beach treasures into my pockets, so I also folded these life lessons into my heart and they have guided me through many of life's rocky shoals.

I believe there's no more wonderful world than the one waiting for me out there by the sea. An hour of beachcombing, of strolling through the silky sand with the sun at my back and the endless blue horizon melting before me, calms my mind as it invigorates my body. I always return home the better for it, with lungs full of fresh air and pockets full of interesting things. The tonic of beachcombing eases me through heartache, leads me to patience and transforms my sometimes tense little life into one of beauty and hope and joy again. Sometimes it even reminds me that the best things in life are often right there before me in the sand.

Tidal changes and storm surges may erase my sandy footprints, but the lessons the sea deposits on my shore and the treasures I pick up on its beaches will always be with me. Let me share them with you. Let's go beachcombing together.

Chapter 1
Sandcastles

Bless each day.

Chesapeake Bay beach treasures include driftwood; oyster, mussel and razor clam shells; chunks of iron ore; sea gull feathers; and horseshoe and blue crab shells.

Chesapeake Bay, Maryland: *Sandcastles*

Bless each day.

Life is a beach. At least, that's what the bumper stickers say. But to my way of thinking, we are the beach. Life is the sea, continually sweeping across us, smoothing or ruffling our shores with the roll of its waves and white caps, its eddies, crosscurrents and undertows, rip tides, spring tides, flood tides. At times restless and churning, then calm and placid, the sea touches us in a continual round of loss and renewal. We progress, regress, lose ourselves, then find ourselves again. Flowing in, then flowing out, the tides of life can defeat or replenish our spirits, dampen or lift our moods, mold, define or burnish our characters. During the wildest storms, waves overwhelm the shore, sweeping in debris and then sweeping it out, leaving us naked and exposed at low tide with once-hidden treasures now revealed.

Since I was a young child, I have turned to the sea and, with the exception of a few miserable years dry-docked at college in Ohio, I've always managed to live a stone's throw away from it. In the early 1950s, when I was a baby, we summered in, and soon after moved to, a small peninsula of land bordered by a lake, an inlet, a river, a creek and Chesapeake Bay. Early memories have me crossing to my first beach down a hydrangea-lined path by our cottage. The path opened to a world of warm sand, warmer sun, sparkling diamonds on the Bay, and an abounding sense of love, light and breeze. I'd paddle my inner tube around my grandmother, the long skirt of her old-fashioned swimming suit splaying out around her like black seaweed.

In my preteen and teen years, I earned pocket money catching and selling blue crabs (a dollar a dozen) and spent long, lazy days on the beach skipping stones, gossiping with girlfriends or watching Dad fish. Over the years, I swam in and out of mermaid palaces forged from rocks, grew hoarse from playing heated games of water tag and Marco Polo, threw sand and seaweed, fell off jetties, sang around bonfires, went skinny dipping, camped out, stepped on broken glass, slimy eels, hot tar and prickly crabs, and had my first real kiss on a Chesapeake Bay beach.

Water is my touchstone. Like a mother, its loyalty is steadfast. When I was a child and there was no one to play with, it entertained me. When I was upset, it comforted me. When life proved disquieting, it calmed me. When I needed to sort things out, it lent perspective. Whenever my emotions threatened to overwhelm me, I knew I could head to the beach, stretch out on the sand and listen to the waves roll in and roll out, roll in and roll out. They sounded like the world breathing. Like Mother Nature's mantra.

For more than half a century, I've walked the beaches of my childhood home. This has nourished a kind of intimacy. I know how the shore sounds in this wind, in this weather, in this season, at this time of day. I am as familiar with the lazy slap of waves on windless days as I am with the slosh of gentle swells on a changing tide. I know the ruffle of dune grass in a spring breeze and the eerie whine of sailboat halyards shuddering in gale force winds. I am driven to distraction by the noisy squawk of gulls fighting for food, and always smile at the merry mallards when they sally forth for crumbs. I know, too, the silence of the heron, the sting of the sea nettle, and the scuttle of the crab as it steals from a net into the dark green loam. Then there are the seasonal patterns so easily distinguished: the windswept winter beach, cold and barren after a nor'easter; the worn-out summer beach, filthy from the trash left by thoughtless bathers; and the glorious autumn and spring beaches, drenched in golden light with a nip in the air.

*"Like sandcastles that face a coming high tide,
my bucketful of early treasures reminds me that life is
brief and that everything is temporary and on loan."*

Chesapeake Bay was the start of my beach life. Treasure hunting here can sweep one back 25 million years or more, from the Miocene Period through early American Indian fishing camps and 17th-century European settlements; from Victorian resorts to present-day summer colonies and suburban neighborhoods. Like most little kids, my first treasures were big and obvious. At the end of the day, my pail overflowed with oyster, clam and mussel shells whose interiors gleamed a silvery purple. Sometimes I'd include stiff gull feathers and chunks of iron ore. Simple things. Easy. Uncomplicated. Like my life back then.

But that simple life is gone, replaced by one far more layered and complex. I've sailed many oceans and lived on many shores, suffered heartbreak, celebrated blessings and tried my best to meet life's challenges. My early years on the beach taught me two important lessons: to trust my instincts and to stay true to myself. Since then, I've learned when to hoist the sails and move on if I venture too far off course or stray into dangerous waters. I've also learned that, just as the shifting sands can devour or expose treasures, so can life's shifting fortunes do the same to me.

Like sandcastles that face a coming high tide, my bucketful of early treasures reminds me that life is brief and that everything is temporary and on loan. Each day is best begun by counting blessings and remembering that, while this time is mine, I should embrace and hold it dear no matter what challenges lay ahead. I hope, when the time comes, I'll be able to let go gently, with grace and gratitude, my beach treasures by my side.

The Consummate Beachcomber

Chesapeake Bay

Chesapeake Bay divides part of Virginia and splits the state of Maryland nearly in half. Covering 2,500 square miles, it is more than 200 miles long and, in some places, nearly 30 miles wide. It has a watershed that drains about 60,000 square miles of land in Washington, D.C. and six states: Maryland, Delaware, Virginia, Pennsylvania, New York and West Virginia.

The Bay's evolution began 35 million years ago, during the late Eocene period, when a series of comets hit the earth so forcefully that parts of its crust were reshaped. This included a 55-mile-wide crater southeast of what is now Washington, D.C., which became the site where the Susquehanna River first flowed downhill into the sea. During this era, the region now covered by Chesapeake Bay was alternately dry land and the floor of Miocene and Eocene coastal seas.

Circumpolar ice caps during the last ice age (10,000 to 2 million years ago) kept masses of seawater frozen and immobile. Because of this, the mid-Atlantic coast was a dry landmass stretching about 180 miles further east than it does today. When the glacier began to melt, sea levels rose as much as 40 inches per century. Rising sea levels eventually overflowed from the Atlantic Ocean and flooded into the Susquehanna River Valley forming what we now call Chesapeake Bay. The Bay evolved into its current shape about 3,000 years ago.

As North America's largest estuary the Bay's spectrum of aquatic environments creates a unique ecosystem teeming with life. In 2,000 BCE semi-nomadic Native American tribes such as the Piscataway, Choptank and Algonquin moved into the area and discovered such an abundance of fish, mollusks and shellfish that the region became a favorite destination known as *Chesepiooc* (Algonquin for "Great Shellfish Bay").

European explorers arrived in the 16th century and, over the next 300 years, established plantations, businesses and towns on the Bay's eastern and western shores. Then, with the introduction of railroads and steamboats after the Civil War, grand Victorian beach resorts were built to accommodate city folk seeking to escape the sweltering summer heat. The popular resorts were soon followed by a proliferation of private camps, yacht clubs and summer colonies, which flourished up and down the Bay. The Chesapeake Bay region, with its peaceful corridors of calm water, low-lying marshes and sandy islets, became known as *The Land of Pleasant Living*.

In the 1950s the demand for permanent housing brought on by the post-WWII baby boom transformed this peaceful way of life as summer communities morphed into year-round suburban neighborhoods. Nowadays, though still a lovely region, pollution, unchecked growth and ill-advised development have seriously threatened the Bay's ecology. Fortunately, public sector and private citizen groups are recognizing the gravity of the situation and are stepping up efforts to save the Bay and its surrounding habitat.

Mollusks and Common Bay Shells

Chesapeake Bay beaches are littered with shells, from horseshoe crabs and blue crabs to oysters, mussels and clams. The latter three shells are bivalves from the phylum *Mollusca*, which is, next to insects, the second largest and most diverse phylum of animals. There are about 100,000 species of mollusks found in nearly every ecosystem in the world, including high mountains, tropical rain forests, grassy plains, and in lakes, rivers, bays and oceans.

The fleshy parts of a mollusk include organs for digestion, circulation, reproduction and respiration. Mollusks also have a foot that provides them with the means to move, and a hard external shell that regulates temperature and protects their spineless, fleshy bodies from harm. These shells grow as the mollusks grow and, thus, remain their home for life. That means a mollusk's shell is never shed until the mollusk dies.

Bivalves such as oysters, clams and mussels, are mollusks with two shells attached by a hinge. These bivalves serve as important food sources for other mollusks and for fish, shore birds and humans. Because bivalves are filter feeders—pumping water through their gills and filtering out excess nutrients—they tend to accumulate pollutants and thus offer a means for scientists to track and monitor water pollution.

Oysters, in particular, play a critical role in the health of Chesapeake Bay for a number of reasons: they filter and clean the water; they build extensive reef systems providing habitat for fish and smaller sea animals; and they serve as a food source for other creatures. A century ago, seasonal harvests of native oysters yielded millions of bushels. Today, pollution and over-harvesting have reduced Chesapeake Bay oyster populations to about one percent of those historic levels.

Chapter 2
Wave Riding

*Obstacles are just
challenges to be overcome.*

*A whelk, a whelk egg case and two
Atlantic moon snails from the Jersey Shore*

Sea Girt, New Jersey: *Wave Riding*

Obstacles are just challenges to be overcome.

My first real foray into beachcombing began during summer vacations on the Jersey Shore. As early as age three, I remember walking hand-in-hand with Mother near the shore break. Occasionally she'd dip down to find a moon shell to show me, or hold a lightning whelk to my ear so I could hear the sounds of waves magically stirring inside it. Today those same shells sit in a glass bowl on my piano.

Mother grew up in Belmar, a small town on the New Jersey coast and, in many ways, she never left it. Every summer she'd cart us north to her sister's home in Sea Girt, a nearby borough. Our yearly holidays at my Aunt's revolved around one thing only—the beach—and every day was spent getting ready for it, playing on it, or coming home from it. Period.

On a typical summer morning, the cooler was already packed with ice, drinks and sandwiches by the time we bounded out of bed. We'd tug on suits, slurp down cereal, retrieve rafts and swim gear and towels slung by the outdoor shower, dump everything into a wagon, argue over who'd pull the wagon, race each other four blocks to the boardwalk, then breathlessly run down the dry, splintery steps to a world of endless possibilities. There, before us, stretched miles of open beach and the gray-blue Atlantic Ocean waiting to be conquered.[1]

But not before my mother and aunt performed familiar rituals. First they'd stake out camp, always, cleverly, near the lifeguard stand. Then they'd spread the towels, pump up our canvas rafts, buckle our *Bubbles* (a popular 1950's flotation device worn around the waist), slop suntan lotion on our backs and zinc oxide on our noses, and warn us to keep an eye on each other and not go out too far. Only then could we fly off to the wild wet yonder while they baked in

---

[1] Barry Cornwall's poem, *The Sea*, succinctly sums up the jolt of happiness that courses through me whenever I sight a large body of water: The sea! The sea!
The open sea!
The blue, the fresh,
The ever free!

the sun reading the latest issue of *Good Housekeeping*. Three hours later, we'd tumble in for a lunch of cream cheese and jelly sandwiches and an intolerably long hour of bickering and card playing waiting for our food to digest. Finally, after reapplying zinc oxide, we'd leap back into the surf for another ecstatic three hours.

Jersey waves break near to shore, which can make getting boiled—tumbled over and over in whitewater—particularly painful. I can still recall the cold panic that gripped me whenever a strong, insistent wave sucked me under and churned me in its bubbly, blinding foam. Then, just as my lungs felt close to bursting, the sea always managed to spit me out onto the sand, where I'd lie as breathless and inert as a beached whale, smarting from the sting of saltwater up my nose.

> *"All day, every day, I'd catch a wave,*
> *get boiled, get beached,*
> *then charge back out for more."*

Often I find life to be like those early ocean swims when seemingly insurmountable obstacles loom so large I cower in their shadows, just as I did with oncoming waves when I was young. Then, as now, my first reaction is always one of panic and confusion. Do I try to outrun the obstacles? Or do I rise to the challenge and face them down, knowing full well they have the potential to break me into bits like broken shells or leave me as exhausted as a wave-tossed child sprawled in the shallows by the shore?

But I learned to love the thrill of the ride too much to stay away from the waves. So, after a brief rest, I'd jump up, grab my raft and head back out. All day, every day: catch a wave, get boiled, get beached, then charge back out for more. Amazingly, I was never seriously hurt. None of us were. Perhaps we were lucky. Or perhaps we learned that tensing up only made matters worse; only made us choke and swallow more water or slam like sledgehammers on the hard ocean floor when waves wiped us out. But if we stayed relaxed, we'd bounce like soft, rubber balls in the frothy backwash.

The lightning whelks and moon snails in my glass bowl remind me of those salty childhood summers when I gained that special confidence that comes from facing adversity and not letting it break me. I kept returning to the waves, not only for the thrill of the ride, but also because I relished rising to the challenge. Conquering the waves, ride by ride, ultimately outweighed my fear of being wiped out by them. When seawater smothered me, I learned to relax instead of panic. To avoid getting boiled, I learned to somersault in the backwash and perfected the technique of diving under the wave until it passed over me. Eventually, handling unruly waves became second nature. Eventually, I learned to master even the biggest waves.

Just like those Jersey Shore waves, too much adversity in the sea of life can wear you down until the safety of the shore becomes preferable to the thrill of the ride. But facing and conquering adversity is liberating. It can make you feel almost as good as catching and riding a perfect wave all the way in to shore.

The Consummate Beachcomber

The Jersey Shore on the Atlantic Ocean

The famed Jersey Shore is a 127-mile stretch of white sand beach situated on the world's second largest ocean, the Atlantic, which was formed more than 165 million years ago. It started as a small trickle of water after a geologic rift split the super continent, *Gondwanaland*, into two separate land-masses known today as South America and Africa. The gradual widening of that watery rift now separates these landmasses—as well as North America and Europe—by more than 2,000 miles. And the Atlantic Ocean is still growing at a rate of about one inch per year.

The Atlantic holds some of the world's most abundant and productive fisheries. That, coupled with the Jersey Shore's benevolent climate and broad sweep of inlets, lakes and ponds, provided a comfortable watering hole for Native American tribes such as the Lenape, Navesink and Minnesink. During the Victorian era, the coast developed a reputation as a pleasure playground for an interesting cross-section of Americans including Presidents, doyens of high society, business moguls, religious groups,[1] and Irish Catholic and Italian immigrant families. Summer visitors lodged in charming cottages or stayed in grand hotels where, when they weren't swimming or promenading up and down the boardwalk, they sat on

[1] One of the more picturesque Jersey Shore communities is Ocean Grove. Founded by a Methodist preacher who sought a meeting site where spiritual and physical health could be renewed, it is now listed on the National Register of Historic Places.

24

the generous verandas reading or playing cards.

The borough of Sea Girt, in Monmouth County, sits squarely in the middle of the Jersey Shore. In the 1800s, because of the numerous boats that shipwrecked in that area, the entire coast of Sea Girt became known as Wreck Pond. To bridge the dark, dangerous waters between Barnegat Inlet and the Navesink Highlands, the Sea Girt Lighthouse was erected in 1896. Today it serves as the town's historical museum.

Shells on Mid-Atlantic Shores

The Jersey Shore offers an abundance of shells for the collector who combs the beach in the right season and at the right time of day. The Atlantic surf clam, the knobbed whelk, channeled whelk and the Atlantic slipper shell are common finds. Other favorites such as the lightning whelk and the common northern moon shell (or *moon snail*) frequently turn up on the shoreline alongside bundles of "snap" sea kelp, dark skate egg sacks (or *mermaid's purses*) and the occasional stray rubber flip-flop.

More than one third of all mollusk species, including the lightning whelk and common northern moon shell, are spineless animals called *gastropods*, which means stomach-footed. Most gastropods are *univalves*; that is, they have a single external shell consisting of a coiled tube wrapped around an imaginary point. Shells form when hatched larvae living on the floor of the ocean secrete calcium carbonate and a protein substance called *conchiolin*. These form a covering around the gastropod that eventually hardens into a shell.[2] As the gastropod grows, so does its shell and, thus, the fleshy animal is always protected by its permanent home.

Like other gastropods, moon shells and lightning whelks have a large, muscular foot that enables them to crawl and move about. Along with the foot, their bodies have other clearly-defined regions including a head, a mantle and a fleshy body mass. The head includes tentacles, eyes and a mouth armed with a rasping tongue called a *radula*. The mollusks use their radula, which feels like sandpaper, to catch and rip apart food. Their *mantle* is a sheet of tissue that covers their body and also secretes the calcium carbonate that forms their shell.

Lightning whelks live in saltwater. Moon shells can live in both fresh and saltwater. No matter where you are in the world—by saltwater or freshwater, atop a mountain, on a barren plain or even crossing a sweltering desert—if you put these shells up to your ear and close your eyes, the sounds of a seaborne wind and crashing waves will reach you.

---

[2]   Mollusks secrete additional layers of calcium carbonate and conchiolin to give their shells more strength. This sometimes produces a mother-of-pearl effect on the inside of the shell.

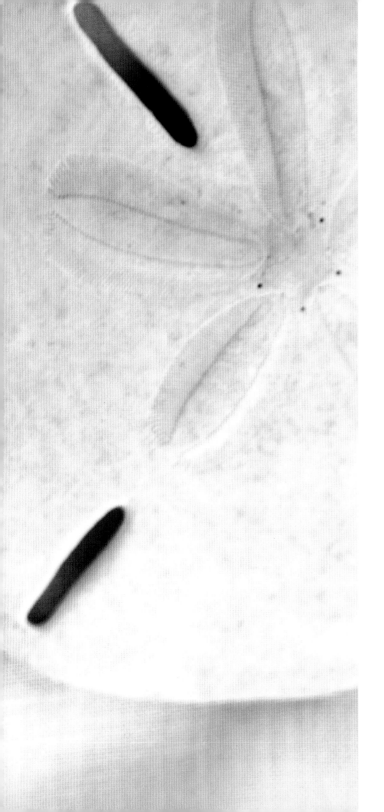

Chapter 3
Pocket Treasure

*Time is your most
precious commodity.*

*A Georgia sand dollar
(also called a keyhole urchin)
beside an antique bottle filled
with silver dimes*

Jekyll Island, Georgia: *Pocket Treasure*

Time is your most precious commodity.

The bus has just stopped in front of the house. School is out. My youngest hops off with a smile. He's had a good day. He lets himself in, wanders into the office and gives me a hug. He has no homework, he says, can we go outside to play? The day is beautiful and I've been writing since early morning. But I'm on a roll. The words are flowing. I tell him to get a snack, practice his saxophone and then we'll see. He is a compliant child and leaves to do my bidding. But I can tell he's disappointed.

A lovely fall sunlight streams into my office illuminating two items on the window ledge: a small bottle filled with silver dimes and a solitary chipped sand dollar. Both came from my father, a great man. Funny. Irreverent. A ball of fire. Always ready with a smile, a joke, a pat on the back, a highball. When I was young, I never got to spend much time with him. During the week, he was busy chasing money and big men's dreams. On weekends, he fished with buddies or coached Little League; so, unless I tagged along, I rarely saw him. But I have two special memories of time spent with Dad. Curiously, both involve money: people money (silver dimes) and beach money (sand dollars).

The dimes in the bottle came from magic tricks he performed when he came home from work each day. The ritual is etched in my mind. At the first sound of tires crunching on the oyster shell drive, I dropped what I was doing and raced to the door with a copper penny in my outstretched hand. I watched Dad climb from the car and walk toward me, smiling. When he reached the doorway, he'd kiss me, take my copper penny and wrap it in a handkerchief. He'd wave the cloth bundle through the air with a flourish before snapping it open to reveal, not an old copper penny, but a shiny-bright silver dime that I promptly retrieved and deposited in my jam jar bank upstairs.

Another moment in time occurred one night when I was six and we were vacationing on Jekyll Island. I was riding in a Jeep with Dad down a dark, spooky, secluded road hemmed in by thick pines. He stopped the car at one point, turned off the lights and motioned to me to be very, very quiet. We sat in the darkness for what felt like an eternity until suddenly, without warning, Dad flipped the headlights back on. There in the road before us stood a magnificent buck, frozen in place, blinking back at the blinding lights. He was a six-point buck. A big, beautiful boy with muscled flanks and a quivering nose, just like the one in fairy tales who stomps his hoof and jewels drop from the sky. Like that story, I blinked once and the buck was gone, vanished back into the night.

Dad continued driving down the road until we reached a deserted beach. He parked, grabbed a flashlight and, following its wide beam, led me toward the sound of waves. Ghost crabs, routed from their seaweed shelters by the light, scurried to the safety of the sea. Dad caught

"Scores of them lay stranded in the sea's foamy backwash,
their brown supple fuzziness blending in with the mocha-colored sand."

and released one, then showed me how to do it, too, without getting pinched. After awhile, we turned our attention to another creature the flashlight revealed: sand dollars. Scores of them lay stranded in the sea's foamy backwash, their brown supple fuzziness blending in with the mocha-colored sand. We selected a few to take back to the hotel and lined them up on a deck railing the next day to whiten in the sun. In my memory, those sand dollars resemble battle-weary soldiers returning home, their khaki uniforms fading into the same brittle white of old bones I sometimes see on the beach.

It's been 30 years since my father's death. Except for some letters and WWII medals, I have only photos and memories to bring him back into my life. The expensive presents he gave me after each business trip are long gone and I have no recollection of the restaurants or fancy parties he took me to. What I do remember cost him little but his time. Time, and the magic of the moment. Of turning copper pennies into silver dimes and showing me the special secrets that nature hides in the stillness of the night: a stunned deer, a feisty crab, and the sublime silence of a sand dollar, all shared with the first man I ever loved.

My son reappears in the doorway holding a football, ready for a game of toss. It's glorious outside and his face is as eager as mine used to be when I thought Dad might play with me. I push back from the desk. I've written enough for the day and I don't want to keep that special person waiting any longer. As I leave the office, I glance at the window ledge and silently thank my father for the gift of time he gave me so many years ago. Beach dimes. Silver dimes. Daddy's dimes. To a child, time—not pocket change—is your most precious commodity.

The Consummate Beachcomber

Jekyll Island

Jekyll Island is one of 13 principal barrier islands strung along 90 miles, north to south off Georgia's coast.[1] Bordered by the Atlantic Ocean on one side and productive tidal marshes on the other, these barrier islands play a critical role in the formation and protection of the state's coastal beaches.

Geologically, barrier islands are regarded as *ephemeral entities* because they disappear and reappear whenever glacial ice sheets expand or retract, thus causing fluctuations in sea levels. When sea levels rise, low-lying coastal areas flood and disappear. When sea levels fall, ridges of coastal sediment are exposed, creating barrier islands. Because sea level change cycles take tens of thousands of years to occur, barrier islands are relatively stable during "still times." Even so, powerful natural forces such as winds, waves, tides, storms and ocean currents can affect their formation and re-shape their contours. Because the *leeward*, or sheltered, sides of barrier islands are shielded from most strong winds, unusually complex intertidal ecoscapes can form. These ecoscapes provide habitats for a host of fascinating plant and animal life.

In the U.S., barrier islands are found along the Gulf Coast and the entire eastern seaboard from Florida to Maine. They range in age from 5,000 to 30,000 years old. Georgia boasts some of the most pristine barrier islands. Of these, Jekyll Island is unique in both location and history. It boasts the westernmost seaport on the eastern seaboard, and is tucked in far enough that most hurricanes bypass it as they make their way north. (At least, that's the theory since the last hurricane to hit the island was in 1898.) The Island's marshes serve as important breeding grounds for shrimp, and Loggerhead turtles still stagger up its beaches to nest and lay their eggs. In the cooling autumn months, marsh grasses turn such a vibrant shade of yellow that Jekyll and adjacent barrier islands are popularly referred to as the *Golden Islands*.

Archaeological evidence suggests that American Indians began visiting Jekyll as early as 2,500 BCE. Legend has it that the island was first occupied by the Timucuan tribe and later the Guale.

[1] Georgia's main barrier islands are Tybee, Little Tybee, Wassaw, Ossabaw, St. Catherines, Blackbeard, Sapelo, Little St. Simons, Sea, St. Simons, Jeykll, Cumberland and Little Cumberland. Some of the islands, such as Wassaw, Blackbeard and Cumberland, are primarily under federal management. Others, such as Ossabaw, Sapelo and Jekyll are managed by the state of Georgia. St. Catherines, Little St. Simons, Sea Island and Little Cumberland are privately owned and managed. Only four barrier islands—Tybee, St. Simons, Sea Island and Jekyll—are connected to the mainland by causeway.

Spanish and French explorers reached the island in the 1500s and it eventually became an outpost of the Spanish Mission system. The Spanish called it the *Isla de Ballenas*, or Whale Island, because its waters were important breeding grounds for right whales. Over the next two centuries English settlers and French planters—along with pirates, renegades and slaves—populated the island. In 1734 the island was named after the English lawyer, Sir Joseph Jekyll,[2] and, in 1791, Frenchman Christophe Poulain du Bignon purchased the island to farm cotton. Then, in 1858, 40 years after the U.S. abolished the importation of slaves, a vessel named *The Wanderer* illegally made port near du Bignon's plantation with what was to be the last cargo of African slaves to America.[3]

At the turn of the century a group of wealthy industrialists purchased the island and established the exclusive Jekyll Island Club. This club served as the social epicenter for America's economic elite for decades. In 1947 the state of Georgia purchased the island and, in 1978, designated it a National Historic Landmark. Today everyone, regardless of economic or social standing, can enjoy Jekyll Island's beautiful beaches.

Sand Dollar

The flat sand dollar is also known as a *keyhole urchin* because of the five slots on its shell. From a class of spiny-skinned marine animals called *echinoids*, sand dollars are related to sea cucumbers, sea stars and sea urchins. When dried, the skeletons of sand dollars resemble large round coins stamped with petal-like patterns in the center. When alive, they resemble brown discs that are covered with a very fine layer of fuzzy hair-like spines, which enable them to burrow into or slowly creep through sand. The holes in a sand dollar are actually pores, internal water-vascular systems that help it move through water.

Sand dollars live just beyond low water, on top of or just beneath the surface of muddy or sandy areas. The best time to collect them is when the tide recedes, or after a heavy storm, because wave action dredges up dead shells.

---

[2] Sir Joseph Jekyll was a supporter of James Oglethorpe, who established the English colony, Georgia, in what is now Savannah.

[3] More than 400 Africans were unloaded that day on Jekyll Island and illegally sold into slavery.

Chapter 4
Watermarks

*When life throws you
a curve ball, bend.*

*American Indian, colonial and Victorian
era artifacts and natural treasures found along
a Chesapeake Bay beach: a glass button,
arrowheads, a molded ceramic rosette, a quartz
seaweed agate and stone-encrusted ore*

Bay Ridge, Maryland: *Watermarks*

When life throws you a curve ball, bend.

Eventually there comes a year in every life when things happen that offer a glimpse into a different world, a colder one, like nothing you've ever known. For me that year came at age nine. But along with this foray into difficult times came three of the best gifts I ever received: a secret beach to call my own; the beginning of a lifelong friendship with myself; and the attitude that hurtful times needn't cripple me if I learn from them.

A Child's Tale

It was going to be another muggy day. My forehead was already wet with perspiration as I leaned over the jetty to catch one last blue crab. Crabbing was how I made pocket money in the summer. If I got out early enough—just after sunrise—Chesapeake Bay was full of crabs. By working each jetty, I could usually catch two or three dozen before breakfast. Selling them at a dollar a dozen meant I'd already made three dollars that morning! I put one dollar aside for the upcoming Jamboree and saved two dollars to treat the Five Fingers to ice cream after lunch.

The Five Fingers were my special group of friends. Every week in the summer one of us had the other four over for lunch. This was our last lunch of the summer and today was my turn. Sara, who was on the pudgy side, was the thumb; Carol Anne, the tiniest, was the little finger; Polly, the bossiest, was the pointer; Jill was the ring finger and, since I was the tallest, I was the middle finger. We'd been friends since kindergarten.

After selling my crabs door-to-door, I walked home and wandered into the kitchen to see Momma.

"Good work, honey," she said, seeing my dollar bills. "You were the early bird today."

"It's my new crab net. It's making me crab better."

"Like new sneakers make you run faster?"

"Yup."

"Well, there's magic in newness sometimes," Momma said. "Now go wash up. The girls will be here soon. And, honey," she called out, "after they've gone, how about we walk down the street to visit a new girl in the neighborhood? Her mother called this morning. The family just moved here and the girl is lonely."

"Okay," I said, but I wasn't much interested.

After lunch, my friends and I went for a long swim in the Bay. Then we sat on the jetty eating ice cream bars I bought from the Good Humor man. When they left, Momma and I went to visit the new neighbors. A woman answered the door. Behind her stood a short, sturdy girl with thick solid legs, stringy brown hair and an engaging, if naughty, grin. I said hello, then followed her upstairs to play. Lucia sure was a different kind of girl. She had a fit of temper when she didn't get her way, but she was also clever and quick and had a good imagination that made even boring games exciting. She also spoke with great authority about things I'd never heard of before, like sperms and eggs and how babies were made. Her ideas sounded so far-fetched I thought she came from Mars. But Lucia was a hard person to resist, and I spent the last week of summer playing with her from morning 'til night.

When school started, I made sure the Five Fingers included Lucia in our games of hopscotch and foursquare. She wasn't good at these games, but she kept up such a stream of smart talk she had all of us laughing, like the time she teased Sheryl Jones about smelling smoky. I knew it was wrong to laugh at Sheryl—her family was going through hard times and relied on a wood stove to heat their house—but, somehow, Lucia made her predicament seem funny.

As the months passed, however, I took to laughing less and less at Lucia's mean jokes. She didn't take kindly to that and soon, the tables turned, and I became one of her victims. Sometimes she mocked my braids or made fun of my freckles. Other times she teased me for playing chase with the boys. She passed notes about me and whispered such rotten things that none of the other girls would play with me, not even the other Five Fingers.

Lucia was a snake and a charmer and all my friends had fallen for her act just like I once had. Not knowing what else to do, I took to sitting by myself on the playground watching everyone else have a good time. Then I'd go home and cry.

"Some people are just mean, honey," Momma told me. "There's no rhyme or reason to it. Don't let her get the better of you. And don't stoop to her level. Your other friends will eventually tire of her, too, like you did. Until then, find different kids to play with and other things to do. Remember, times like these build character."

I tried hard to follow Momma's advice and make new friends at school, but everybody already had their special group. At recess, I took to staying inside helping the teacher clean blackboards or return library books, or else I just sat at my desk reading. I'd never taken the time to read much before, but now I couldn't get enough of *Nancy Drew* or *Anne of Green Gables*. At home, I helped Momma with chores or shot baskets with my brother. Sometimes I played with younger kids on our block. Usually, though, I just kept to myself, reading or taking the dogs for runs on the beach. Still, I was pretty miserable. Building character was no fun.

One day over Easter break Momma suggested we go exploring. She packed a picnic lunch and we trudged toward the steep cliffs towering above the Bay. I followed as she wove her way down a hillside path to a long thin ridge of land wedged between cliff and water. We walked that ridge slowly, shoving aside shoulder-high grasses and briar vines and stepping carefully on a mud trail pocked with raccoon, fox and possum prints.

The ridge widened into a stretch of small beaches broken up by old wooden jetties. Momma stepped down onto one beach and laid out lunch while I sifted through piles of stones by the water. I'd never seen so many pretty stones before: thin, oval quartz; pieces of granite flecked with mica; and agates with veins of black sand running though them. That day produced two incredible treasures: an Indian arrowhead with the tip still intact, and a broken piece of china with the letters "Bay Ri" on it. Momma said the china came from the days when Bay Ridge was a famous Victorian resort known as *The Queen Resort of the Chesapeake*.

"That's quite a find. It must be at least 70 years old," she said.

I hadn't felt this good in a long time and decided to visit what I nicknamed "Stone Harbor" every chance I got. Several times a week, after school, I'd stuff a water canteen and a snack in my knapsack, wave "so long" and head off to the cliffs.

Those afternoons at Stone Harbor helped me get on with life as nothing else had. Besides instilling in me a love for beachcombing, they also awakened my sense of wonder in the world.

I developed favorite rituals for each season. In summer, after a swim, I'd close my eyes and stretch out on the hot planks of the jetty, listening to the *stinkpots* (crab boats) chug along the channel. In the fall, bundled in a sweatshirt, I'd sit on the sand watching the wavering V formations of Canada Geese swimming south, their haunting, melancholy honking heralding the coming of cold, dark days. In winter, when the Bay was partially frozen, I'd toss bread-crumbs to the ducks and laugh as they skittered across the slippery ice toward them. And in spring, when the water was cool and clear, I'd wade in the shallows searching for special stones.

By the time sixth grade started, some of the Five Fingers had tired of Lucia's ways and began drifting back to me. But I had other friends now, like Lenora, who lived on my street. Even though she was two years younger, she was fun to play with and wasn't always looking over her shoulder for a better opportunity. I still kept busy at Stone Harbor, too, and, by the end of that school year, had added another arrowhead, more ceramic shards, some porcelain buttons, a ceramic rosette and a seaweed agate to my collection.

"In summer, after a swim, I'd close my eyes and stretch out on the hot planks of the jetty, listening to the stinkpots (crab boats) chug along the channel."

More important than the treasures was the peace I found inside myself. Stone Harbor taught me to appreciate my own company, to enjoy lying alone in the hot sun, drying off after a dip, with the waves slapping on the jetty and the cries of the gulls overhead. I learned to look more carefully at everything: how the plants changed with the seasons; how the small pink buds of wild roses in the late spring bloomed magenta in the summer, then turned a brittle rust come fall; and how the early winter cliffside, with little more than bare vines and dried grass, trans-formed by June into a hedgerow thick with flowers, butterflies and bumblebees.

Mostly I learned that, when hurtful times come, it's best to look beyond the present pain to new possibilities. Stone Harbor showed me those possibilities. It was there that I found a sense of wonder and of purpose and an opportunity to know myself. Looking back now, what more could a kid ask for? In some ways, I guess I owe that mean ol' martian, Lucia, my thanks.

The Consummate Beachcomber

Bay Ridge on Chesapeake Bay

Bay Ridge is an historic peninsula community located just south of Annapolis where the Severn River meets the Chesapeake Bay. Bordered on two sides by long stretches of beach broken up by cliffs, this resource-rich area has been a favored location for a series of diverse population groups over the last several thousand years.

Ten thousand years ago, American Indian hunter/gatherers roamed the area, using spears fitted with flaked stone points to stalk great Pleistocene mammals. Two thousand years ago, during the Woodland Period, peaceful Indians[1] speaking an Algonquin dialect moved into the area. Attracted by the sheltered forests, wildlife and bountiful sea resources, they set up seasonal camps.[2] By the 1500s incursions of aggressive Susquahannock Indians from the northern Bay region drove the more placid Algonquin-Piscataway tribes down to southern Maryland.

In 1608, on his voyage up the Bay, famed English explorer John Smith noted Bay Ridge's tree-lined shores abundant with game. Beginning with Thomas Tolly in 1650, the peninsula passed through the hands of a succession of people including Richard Hill, whose descendant and heir, Henrietta Margaret Hill Ogle was the wife of Benjamin Ogle, Governor of Maryland from 1798 to 1801. In 1832 the land was bequeathed to Maria Lloyd Key Steele, daughter of Francis Scott Key, composer of America's national anthem. From the 1670s to about 1840 the property was never owner-occupied. Instead, tenant farmers, slaves and possibly free blacks lived on the land and worked the plantation.

In the late 1800s the Steele family began selling off portions of the property. Soon after, a business conglomerate transformed Bay Ridge into a Gay Nineties vacation resort. The resort included dance pavilions, a gravity train, a bandstand and a hotel with a covered pier. City folk from Annapolis, Baltimore and Washington, D.C. traveled to the popular resort by steamboat and train. By 1904, however, the resort had closed and in 1915 the hotel burned down.

---

[1]   They were probably members of the Piscataway tribe.

[2]   In this part of Maryland, the lack of resident American Indian tribes resulted in few rivers and creeks with Indian names (i.e., Severn, South and West Rivers, and Back, Weems and College Creeks).

The abandoned property was purchased by a group of investors who formed the Bay Ridge Reality Company. The land was surveyed, divided into saleable plots and advertised throughout the region as the perfect place for a summer holiday.

Within five years, more than 100 families owned vacation bungalows on the peninsula and Bay Ridge thrived as a summer colony. The increased housing demands brought on by WWII encouraged families to winterize and live in the cottages year round. Though the community still has some summer-only residents, like other well-known Chesapeake summer colonies—Sherwood Forest, Highland Beach, North Beach and Scientist Cliffs—Bay Ridge is now home to hundreds of year-round residents who enjoy its beauty, tranquility and neighborliness.

Chesapeake Bay Artifacts

The succession of visitors to Chesapeake Bay shores—American Indians to colonial farmers, Victorian vacationers to summer sailors—has created an ideal environment in which to find a range of fascinating man-made artifacts. Over the years, beachcombers have discovered arrowheads, glass buttons, stamped bottles, Civil War bullets, pieces of porcelain and stoneware, clay pipes, marbles, iron implements and sections of railroad track. Old garbage heaps, or *middens*, of discarded clam and oyster shells indicate the presence of Indians in the area thousands of years ago. Occasionally, chunks of charred brick, melted glass and square nails, residue from the hotel fire nearly a century earlier, turn up on various beaches.

Arrowheads, probably made and used by Algonquin or Susquehannock Indians several centuries ago, are rare beach finds. The ones that I found as a child are still intact and very sharp. Archaeological speculation about the sandstone rosette ranges from a colonial architectural piece to a decorative prize offered during Victorian resort days. The distinctive blue-flowered bordered plates were part of a signature collection of hotel china used during that same era.

Chapter 5
Beach Bugs

Play every day.

A sea star (starfish), sea glass and several different types of shells (murex, miter and a sea worm shell) planted on a Florida beach by the author's grandfather

Key Biscayne, Florida: *Beach Bugs*

Play every day.

I'd heard about it for years but now vague signs start to appear. A gray hair here. A permanent brow furrow there. A certain sluggishness of spirit and a mild dissatisfaction with life. Some days feeling restless and edgy, others like I'm wading through quicksand, my body so slow, my thoughts so vague.

Midlife. What a ride. I hadn't a clue how best to wend my way through the physical and emotional upheavals that come with this stage of life.

Then, one day, it came to me. Play! Life had become far too serious with all the household, family, financial and professional demands. I hadn't had a belly laugh in months or let loose and done something silly. I'd read an article once about the importance of play to child development. Play stretches physical and mental muscles and teaches children crucial skills: how to get along with others, how to use their imagination, how to relax. Unfortunately, as we age, the concept of play as a critical part of our well-being somehow gets lost on the road to maturity. I'd wager that, as most of us enter midlife, we feel less inclined to laugh or do spontaneous things or experience that joyful sense of abandon we had as children. This can make for a dull old life.

Two things got me up and moving again. Both were activities I loved to do in my youth. The first was triggered by the purchase of a fire-engine red bike at a yard sale. This was not a bells-and-whistles type bike with 20 gears and an aerodynamic, micro-foam padded seat. This was a generic beach bike with foot brakes, large tires and no fenders or gears. If I attached a bell and basket, pinched playing cards to the spokes with wooden clothespins and strung streamers from the handlebars, it'd be the exact same bike I had when I was 10.

Riding the bike was reflexive and not an intellectual exercise. Just pedal, steer and brake. Every time I careened down a hill, I was 10 years old again, zigzagging back and forth, feet splayed out, head thrown back, a bouquet of summer scents—fresh cut grass, privet, honey-suckle—tickling my nose. Windblown. Laughing. Liberated. People thought I looked silly. But who cared? I'm 10! It's okay to look silly.

A few weeks later, I watched some kids digging tunnels in the sand and remembered how much I used to like to dig tunnels and build sandcastles. I especially liked to build bug cabanas. Pop-pop taught me how to make those the year we visited him in Florida when I was 11. He must have been about 70. A spry 70. Fleet of foot, with a twinkle in his eye. And probably still up to his usual tricks, like quickly slipping his false teeth out of his mouth during dinner when I was the only one looking. Caught off guard, I'd laugh so hard I'd sometimes snort milk from my nose. While everyone's attention was turned toward the mess I'd made, Pop-pop innocently resumed eating. Minutes later, however, if he caught my eye, he'd wink and slip his dentures out again.

That trip to Florida marked my introduction to the tropics. I remember it as a riot of neon colors and sweet, sweet smells: bright plastic juice-filled oranges with emerald straws; snow globes with hot pink flamingos; and yellow bananas, lime green coconuts, orange blossom perfume, cream-colored gardenias and coconut tanning oil. Even the ocean—a dreamy turquoise—and shells in shades of rose, purple and gold were far more colorful than anything I was accustomed to up north.

Pop-pop lived in a modest, avocado-green stucco house surrounded by palm trees and bougianvillea. He had a shady courtyard where we played Canasta during the heat of the day. Afterward, we'd go to a nearby club to swim in its grotto-like pool with mini-waterfalls. This relaxing holiday suited my parents perfectly, but I yearned to beachcomb for pretty shells like the ones I'd seen in the gift shop at South of the Border, an over-the-top, bubblegum-colored motel where we overnighted on the drive down.

I realize now that Pop-pop knew the best shelling beaches were hundreds of miles northwest on the Gulf Coast but, to his credit, he took me beachcombing anyway. We drove to a beach on Key Biscayne[1] and spent hours walking up and down the shoreline. I found one starfish and some seed pods but there were hardly any pretty shells; at least not like the ones in the saran-wrapped baskets at South of the Border. (Probably because those were imported from the Philippines.)

To cheer me up, Pop-pop suggested we build bug cabanas.

---

[1]   *Key* is the Americanized version of the Spanish word cayo which means "small island."

"What for?" I asked.

"To keep the bugs from getting sunburned, of course," he said.

Intrigued, I jumped up to help him collect stuff—feathers, twigs, seaweed, bottle caps—that we used to build and decorate the structure. Then we scoured the beach for bugs, dumping them unceremoniously into the cabana, and sat down to watch the miniature circus unfold. Bugs climbed on walls and "sat" on "sofas." They congregated on the roof and bumped into each other in "doorways." One beetle even slept on the "dining table!"

As always, Pop-pop transformed a disappointing day into a light-hearted romp. Was his ability to reach for joy no matter what the circumstances a learned trait or an inherent one? Perhaps being a young drummer boy in the bloody Spanish-American War, or losing everything in the Great Depression, or living through two horrific World Wars, taught him to seek the "silver lining through the dark clouds shining" [2] as a means of survival. Or maybe he was just blessed with an easy temperament. Whichever, he paid scant attention to nay-sayers, finger waggers, eyebrow raisers or "titch-titchers" because life was short, dadgummit, and his life was going to be as sweet as it could be. Poet .e. e. cummings sweetly summed up Pop-pop's philosophy:

> *you shall above all things be glad and young*
> *for if you're young, whatever life you wear*
>
> *it will become you; and if you are glad*
> *whatever's living will yourself become…*
>
> *…i'd rather learn from one bird how to sing*
> *than teach ten thousand stars how not to dance* [3]

[2] My mother often sang this stanza of the popular WWI song *Darling Belle* (also known as *'Til the Boys Come Home)* written in 1914 with lyrics by Lena Ford, and music by Ivor Novello.

> Keep the home fires burning
> Though your heart is yearning
> Though your lads are far away
> They dream of home.
> There's a silver lining
> Through the dark clouds shining
> Turn the dark cloud inside out
> Til the boys come home.

[3] From the e.e. cummings poem, *you shall above all things be glad and young*

At Pop-pop's insistence, we returned to the beach a few days later but when we got there, I was more interested in building bug cabanas than in beachcombing. I finally gave in to his urgings and followed him up the shoreline. I kept lagging behind, though, because there were so many pretty shells! By the end of our walk, my pockets bulged with them. Years later I realized Pop-pop had seeded the beach with shells from his own collection including an orange spotted miter, which didn't even come from that region of the world (but who knew?).

Later, during my teen years, when there wasn't much else to do, I'd go to the beach and build bug cabanas. I relished the challenge of relying only on my imagination and the materials at hand to make something out of nothing. Sometimes, the dwellings evolved into elaborate affairs replete with miniature rock walls, oyster shell gates, woven dune grass mats, seaweed beds and stone chimneys.

Thinking back on those days, I decide to take advantage of the balmy spring weather and walk to the beach to build my first bug cabana in 30 years. I spend an hour searching for just the right combination of rocks, iron ore, feathers, shells and beach glass. When I finish the structure, two little girls help me capture ladybugs to populate it. Then we stretch out on our tummies, chins propped on our hands, and giggle as the bugs make themselves quite at home.

Midlife feels many miles away.

The Consummate Beachcomber

Key Biscayne

Key Biscayne is a low-lying, sub-tropical island just south of Miami Beach with 7.5 square miles of beaches, mangrove forests and wetlands. It is the southernmost sand barrier island of the continental U.S. and comes with a fascinating history of Spanish shipwrecks, pirates, and American Indian and military skirmishes.

At the end of the ice age, around 12,000 BCE, the Florida peninsula was twice the size it is today. PaleoIndians roamed the area hunting saber-toothed tigers, mastodons and giant armadillos. Around 5,000 BCE Key Biscayne became a leading settlement site for Tequesta Indians who traveled there in dugout canoes and built permanent fishing villages of stilted dwellings raised above sea level. A hunter/gatherer people, the Tequesta subsisted on diets of fish, mollusks, shellfish, berries, raccoon and snails.

In 1513 famed Spanish explorer Juan Ponce de Leon reached the island, christened it *Santa Marta* and claimed it for the Spanish King. During the 1700s the island was traded back and forth between Spain and England until, by the end of the French and Indian War (also known as the *Seven Years War*), Key Biscayne[1] came under British control. Then, in 1783, with the signing of the Treaty of Paris ending the American Revolution, Spain was allowed to reoccupy Florida in return for its assistance to the colonies. But in 1814, and again in 1816 during the Seminole Wars, U.S. military forces invaded Florida and finally wrenched control of it from the Spanish in 1821.

To protect the island from warring Seminole Indians, the U.S. military soon moved in and built a hospital and a fort. Hoping to stem the number of shipwrecks on outlying reefs, the military constructed a lighthouse in 1825. Eleven years later, the lighthouse was attacked and burned by Indians, but the structure survived and today, the Cape Florida Lighthouse is the oldest standing structure in Miami-Dade County.

When the war ended, surveyors and planters from the north arrived to develop and farm the island. Florida gained statehood in 1845 and by the start of the 20th century Key Biscayne boasted the largest coconut plantation in the U.S., with more than two thirds of the island under cultivation. Regarded as a tropical paradise to rival the islands in the South Seas, Key Biscayne became a popular winter gathering spot for many of America's ruling elite.

Today, beachcombers peruse the shoreline of Bill Baggs Cape Florida State Park, located on the island's southern tip where Biscayne Bay meets the Atlantic Ocean. Each year the park welcomes thousands of visitors who come to explore, fish, boat, swim, stroll along 1.2 miles of beach and even climb the historic lighthouse for a spectacular view of south Florida. They may also see Loggerhead turtles that frequently nest there.

Sea Stars (Starfish)
There is not much to find on Key Biscayne beaches, especially compared to the array of exotic shells found on the shores of its gulf coast neighbors, Sanibel[2] and Captiva Islands. Bits of sea sponge and small pieces of driftwood are sometimes available, as is the occasional sea biscuit or sea star (popularly known as *starfish*). Some people also collect sea pods (or *sea beans*), which are really

---

[1] There are several theories about the naming of Key Biscayne. One theory holds *Biscayne* is a variant on the Bay of Biscay located in the north Atlantic Ocean west of France and north of Spain. The island could also be named after El Biscaino, a man from the Spanish province, Biscaya, whose ship wrecked near the island.
[2] According to Chuck and Debbie Robinson, authors of *The Art of Shelling*, many beachcombers rank Sanibel as one of the top 10 shelling beaches in the world and the best in the Western Hemisphere.

seed pods. Called *Monkey Ladder Pods*, these seeds grow on Monkey Ladder vines that hang from trees in the canopy of Central American jungles. The pods eventually fall, get washed in to the ocean, and some eventually drift northward on the Gulf Stream toward Florida.

The numbers of sea stars increase as you head farther north up the Atlantic coast. Like other *Echinoderms* ("spiny skin" in Greek), sea stars are simple creatures that lack brains but have complex sensing organs. Their bodies are divided into five appendages, each pointing outward from the center. Sea stars also have a unique plumbing system consisting of a hydraulic network of canals that end in a series of tube feet. If you turn a sea star over, you will see the tube feet arranged in rows on each appendage. These feet can extend and contract to propel the sea star through water. They can also catch and grasp prey such as worms, bivalves and crustaceans, and are strong enough to pull apart the tightly clasped shells of bivalves.

A sea star sunbathes by sunburned sea glass.

Chapter 6
Storm Warnings

Forwarned is forearmed.

Assorted pieces of driftwood in the shape of a walking cane, a camel (or an elephant or dragon) and (center) a duck (or guppy or timid rabbit) depending on your point of view

49

Stinson Beach, California: *Storm Warnings*

Forewarned is forearmed.

There is a powerful, primal quality to the beaches of the Pacific Northwest. These are wild, bold shorelines. Elemental. Forceful. Masculine. Beaches that stir the spirit and invigorate the body, the sea fronting them a powerful churning wash of turbulent, ash-gray water.

Stinson, just north of San Francisco, is one such place. Unlike the loose, crazy, anything-goes beaches of southern California, there's nothing soft about Stinson Beach. It offers beachgoers a robust stretch of dun-colored sand under brooding skies. A bracing environment though not a particularly relaxing one. Too many dangers lurk beneath its cold, dark waters: great white sharks, icy currents, undertows so strong they can suck you out to sea in seconds. I was taught early in life that the best way to fend off trouble is to avoid it in the first place. When I visit Stinson, or any beach along the famous *Red Triangle*, I exercise caution, keep my guard up and listen to my instincts. (Fortunately for people with poor instincts, warning signs are posted everywhere...)

The Pacific was in a violent temper the day I first visited Stinson, pummeling the shore with unruly waves. It was a blustery, overcast morning and seabirds flew hard against the wind. Few people braved the beach that day. An adult and child walking hand-in-hand. A surfer in his wetsuit standing nonchalantly by his upright board. A couple struggling to rescue their dog, which was caught in turbulent, muzzle-high backwash. When the dog finally reached the shore, tail wagging, it still had a tennis ball clamped in its mouth.

I kept my distance from the water, preferring instead the upper reaches of the beach where hundreds of dried black egg sacks and some large limpet shells were stranded. Also strewn about were pieces of smooth, silvery driftwood. I love the way driftwood feels and looks, and I have a collection of special pieces gathered from my childhood. Like finding castles in clouds or faces in stones, my pieces of driftwood hold images, too: a turbaned genie, a dromedary camel, a whale, even one that resembles the face of my old dog Mudge. On Stinson I found another piece to add to my collection. From one angle it looked like a guppy, or perhaps a timid rabbit with flattened ears, and from the other like a long-billed duck.

The moodiness of the day, the turbulence of the elements and my new piece of driftwood took me back to times in my childhood when bad storms blew in across the bay from Baltimore. Times when I'd see my shadow suddenly disappear in the sand and, looking skyward, watch as grim, soot-colored, mile-high thunderheads moved in, their heaviness sweeping the sun from the sky and sucking the air from the earth. The Bay always knew a storm was coming, too. She'd flatten her surface into marbled steel as if, by turning inward, she could better fortify herself against the coming onslaught of rain, wind and lightning.

I learned early on that thunderstorms are dangerous. When they threaten, it's time to swim for shore, take down the sails, fire up the motor or seek shelter off the playing field. Ignoring signs of an approaching thunderstorm—like ignoring shark warnings posted on Stinson Beach—is like playing Russian Roulette with Mother Nature.

"These are wild, bold shorelines. Elemental. Forceful. Masculine."

Some neighbors disregarded storm warnings while others grew overly fearful. With hurricanes, my parents practiced a *forewarned-is-forearmed* approach to storm management. The pantry was stocked with food. Chests held enough blankets and drawers enough batteries for the transistor radio and matches for the candles. Dad stacked wood by the fireplace. Mom filled tubs with water.

By anticipating and preparing in advance for potential dangers, inclement weather rarely caught us off guard. We enjoyed the excitement of the storm when it hit. Lightning was beautiful. Torrential rains, thrilling. Strong winds, invigorating. Lost electricity simply meant fun nights of candlelit board games, flashlight hide-and-seek or curling together like spoons under the comforters. These are some of my best childhood memories.

I know it isn't possible to hide from all of life's storms. But I can try to steer clear of them just as I steer clear of the ocean at Stinson Beach. When that isn't possible then I'll turn inward like the Bay and hope that sufficient preparation will get me through until the world rights itself.

On Stinson, the winds are picking up and rain clouds moving in. I'm the last one on the beach. Time to take my piece of driftwood and head for shelter.

The Consummate Beachcomber

Stinson Beach on the Pacific Coast

The majestic Pacific Ocean, *or Mare Pacificum* in Latin, was named by Portuguese explorer Ferdinand Magellan and means "Peaceful Sea." Although its peacefulness is sometimes questionable, everything about the Pacific is big. It is the deepest and largest ocean on earth, reaching a depth of 36,000 feet and covering more square miles than the total land area of the world. It is also the most violent ocean with typhoons, active volcanoes and tidal waves. Because of its depth, *tsunami* (waves created by earthquakes) can reach speeds that rival the same velocity as a jet airplane with heights rivaling eight story buildings. (The tallest wave, recorded in 1933 by the U.S. Navy, was 112 feet!)

Stinson is a 3.5-mile stretch of beach located on the Pacific just 37 miles north of San Francisco. It marks the northernmost point of the infamous *Red Triangle*, a region of the Pacific Ocean known for an abnormally high number of shark attacks. The triangle stretches from San Francisco and Stinson Beach west to the Farallon Islands and south to Big Sur just below Monterey Bay. Great white sharks cruise up and down the region's cold waterways seeking out their favorite foods: elephant seals and sea lions, which reside there in large numbers.

The water at Stinson is chilly year round. Even in summer, the temperature is sometimes too cold for a swim without a wetsuit. But the beach offers day-trippers the perfect place to picnic after viewing the massive Sequoias at nearby Muir Woods National Forest. And Point Reyes National Seashore, located nearby, boasts more than 70 miles of trails where visitors are welcome to picnic, hike, bike, tour the Point Reyes Lighthouse (erected in 1870) or watch the yearly migrations of gray, humpback and blue whales. Migrations of the gray whales, the most commonly seen *cetecean* (dolphins, porpoises, whales) off Stinson, begin each November when they leave the Arctic Ocean and Bering Sea for Baja, Mexico to birth their young. Peak sightings usually occur during January and March. Sitings of humpback and blue whales (the largest animals ever to live on earth) are most frequently seen in the summer and fall months.

Driftwood

Large limpet shells, rocks and driftwood are common finds on Stinson Beach. *Driftwood* refers to pieces of wood weathered over time by sun, saltwater, sand and wave action. The most coveted pieces are those that are a smooth silvery gray or brown and display artistic or anthropomorphic features. Driftwood is used in beach bonfires, furniture making, arts and crafts, or for artistic display. Chemically treated wood such as building timbers or telephone poles do not weather well or take on the lyrical quality of driftwood derived from trees and shrubs. (And the fumes emitted from treated wood when it is burned are dangerous to breathe, so avoid using it in bonfires.)

"Like finding castles in clouds or faces in stones, my pieces of driftwood held images, too: a turbaned genie, a dromedary camel, a whale, even one that resembled the face of my dog Mudge."

A regal bust of my favorite childhood dog, Molly Mudge, a German short-haired pointer.

Chapter 7
Pearly Shells

*Good memories
brighten dark days.*

*Scallop shells and jingle shells from
the quiet shores of Nantucket*

Nantucket Island, Massachusetts: *Pearly Shells*

Good memories brighten dark days.

Spotting an island from the deck of a ship is always a thrill. From that first hazy speck on an otherwise blank horizon to the slow evolution of a recognizable landmass, finding islands at sea is like finding treasure in the sand. Beachcombing for giants.

I've collected quite a few islands in my lifetime. Nugget-sized tropical islands studded with palm trees. Swampy bay islets of little more than marsh grass and duck blinds. Dark, foreboding volcanic islands rising from the ocean's depths. Stoic maroon mounds of peat nestled in the cold North Sea and Moorish-flavored Mediterranian outcrops of caves and scrub brush. Even so, the charm of Nantucket Island as seen from the upper deck of a ferry is unforgettable.

It was the summer before my freshman year of college. Along with some high school friends, I ferried over from Woods Hole to visit a schoolmate summering there. Nearing the island, I saw miles and miles of white sand beach. As we rounded Brandt Point and entered the harbor, Nantucket town appeared, looking just like the 19th-century whaling port it once was. Widows' walks, weather vanes and church steeples marked the skyline. The harbor before me was dotted with boats and buoys and lobster pots. On the main pier a crowd waited patiently to greet guests and family coming off the ferry. Some people balanced on bicycles. Others leaned on pier poles. Everyone appeared tanned, healthy and relaxed. I couldn't wait to join them.

I visited many wonderful beaches that first Nantucket summer. On Siasconset's wild rose and kelp-strewn shoreline, I watched curious seals beyond the breakers stare back at me. I bodysurfed waves on windswept Nobadeer, slid down dunes at Dionis and sunned in sleepy Wauwinet. But the beach that stole my heart was Pocomo. Nearly 40 years later, whenever I think of it, I feel the warmth of its sunshine.

If beaches have personalities, and I believe they do, Pocomo was a well-loved, happy, fresh-faced child. In the early 1970s the village of Pocomo was a collection of small, unpretentious bluff cottages overlooking a bay ringed by barren barrier beaches. No debris marred the shoreline. No blaring radios, noisy cars, fussy children or weary parents. Just the sea, the dune grass, sand bars, an occasional burst of laughter and cotton-puff clouds rolling along in the crayon-blue sky.

Sailboats moved swiftly across the breezy bay that first summer day and sunburned children dug for quahogs in the sandbar. The salt from the sea air stung my lips and the scent of suntan lotion smelled heavenly as I smoothed it on my warm skin. I didn't notice much else, though. My attention was taken up by the person lying next to me.

"In the shallows, luminous jingle shells sparkled by my feet."

When I finally did get up, I wandered along a tideline sprinkled with scallop shells. Their orange-yellow colors and linear designs looked like sun rays stroking the day awake. In the shallows, luminous jingle shells sparkled by my feet. In iridescent, ethereal shades of pearl, butterscotch and melon, they looked like clouds at dawn. Like my world back then. A world that was opening me up in so many new and wonderful ways. A world touched by light.

Love can do that.

Unlike the rest of Nantucket, Pocomo has suffered few growing pains over the last several decades. Even with more houses and increased foot traffic, a summer day there is still as easy, calm and uncomplicated as it was on my first visit. Though that relationship ended years ago, the memories I made that day and the shells I found remain forever mine.

Sometimes on dark days I think back to that time—a Pocomo kind of time—when it was enough just "to be alive," as Bernard Gunther writes, "to see the sea, the sky and watch the changes; to eat, talk, joke, and create, love, feel the air, ground, yourself, and not have to be somebody." A time when the blessing of light touched me both inside and out, and there were fewer responsibilities to tarnish the shine.

The Consummate Beachcomber

Nantucket Island

The island of Nantucket is located 30 miles off the southern coast of Cape Cod, Massachusetts. Shaped like a curved arrow, the 490-square-mile island was formed by the last great North American glacier. The northern part of Nantucket is considered *terminal moraine*,[1] with small hillocks and kettle ponds, while the southern half, formed as the outwash plain of the glacier, is much smoother.

[1] Ridge-like accumulation of glacial debris pushed forward and dumped at the edge of ice advances

Dangerous shoals surround the island and navigating its waters can be risky. The easternmost village, Siasconset, is the closest point in the U.S. to Europe (2,000 miles across the Atlantic Ocean is Portugal).

Though seasonal groups of other Native Americans traveled there to fish, the island's original inhabitants were the Wampanoag who lived there undisturbed for centuries. The name *Nantucket* is Wampanoag for "Faraway Island" or "Land Far Out to Sea." The island is often referred to as *The Grey Lady* because of the mist that frequently enshrouds it.

The first documented sighting of Nantucket was in 1602 by English Captain Bartholomew Gosnold. In 1649 several English families moved there to escape religious persecution on the mainland. In the early 1700s Nantucket became a refuge for Quakers whose austerity and simplicity had a marked influence on island affairs and architecture over the next two centuries.

In the 18th century, when it was discovered that whale oil was an excellent source for lighting and lubrication, Nantucket's maritime colony rose to the challenge, building a fleet of seaworthy vessels capable of sailing its seamen thousands of miles around the globe to hunt the mighty sperm whale. Nantucket came to dominate America's whaling industry in the late 18th and early 19th centuries and became known as the "whaling capital of the world." To pass the time at sea, sailors carved scrimshaw figures from whalebone and wove beautiful baskets from reeds, traditional art forms still popular today. By 1850 a decline in whale populations and the discovery of petroleum put a swift end to Nantucket's golden era. Its population declined and it reverted to its original fishing and farming culture. The island remained a sleepy backwater until recreational boating and tourism took hold in the 1890s. Summer colonies were established and hotels were built to house visitors seeking fresh sea air and saltwater cures.

By the 1950s Nantucket's charm, generous beaches and pleasant summer weather encouraged vacationers to construct more summer homes. Today, Nantucket's winter population of 12,000 swells to 60,000 every summer with visitors who come to stroll the island's cobblestone streets and explore its 82 miles of beaches.

The village of Pocomo is tucked away on a road off Nantucket's increasingly beaten track. Situated on Nantucket Sound, the beach is part of a series of sheltered bays bordered by two National Wildlife Preserves: Cotue and Great Point. With few waves, warm water, gentle breezes and a generous sandbar at low tide, Pocomo is a calm, quiet place to go for a relaxing day of shelling, swimming, sailing and kayaking.

Scallop Shells

Nantucket's ocean beaches are home to whelks, Atlantic surf clams, mermaid purses, driftwood and kelp. Both the colorful Atlantic jingle shells and Atlantic bay scallops are found in abundance along the shore of the island's inner bay.

The scallop, a bivalve, lives in shallow water, usually where eel grass is present. Scallops are shaped like wide-open fans with sculpted ribs radiating outward. They can grow as large as three inches and come in a wide range of colors and designs. Unlike other bivalves, scallops do not burrow into the sand but, instead, lie on the sea bottom. Around the edge of the scallop's mantle are a series of blue eyes that, though rather weak, can detect movement nearby and warn of the presence of predators, particularly the feared sea stars.

Found worldwide, scallops are one of the most popular shells to be photographed, drawn or used in artistic or creative designs. They are also a prized seafood with a mild sweet taste and a firm texture.

An ivory imposter (far right) nestles amongst a bevy of sun-kissed beauties.

Chapter 8
Wind Wakes

Move beyond borders.

*A collection of antique ceramic shards
found on beaches throughout the world*

Runaway Bay, Jamaica: *Wind Wakes*

Move beyond borders.

Beachcombing is a liberating pastime. Meandering along a shoreline looking for treasure provides a break from my worries and the daily routine. It also helps me move beyond the borders—wealth, race, politics, religion—we use to separate us from our common humanity. Beachcombers, generally a friendly bunch, cross these borders regularly to share information and compare or trade artifacts. Our common interests transcend our differences.

The beach, in general, is a great equalizer. No matter what the season, being on a stretch of shoreline always seems to bring out the best in people. Biases evaporate. Defenses are lowered. We forget ourselves and relax. In no time, we catch waves or build sandcastles together. Exchange shells or fishing lures. Share sunblock or even phone numbers. No one cares about your lineage at the beach, or the amount of money you make, or who you worship, or if you're wearing the latest fashion. Maybe world leaders should convene on a beach. They might return home having made fewer rules and fewer wars and probably feeling a lot better about themselves.

During the genteel 1950s and early 60s—my growing up years—I didn't think much about people's differences. Concepts such as religious preferences, social standing, skin color or income level didn't mean anything to me. I never noticed that people from different ethnic and racial groups led polite but separate lives outside of work and school. I never wondered why my best friend in 5th grade returned home to her black neighborhood from my white one after our play dates. Or why Catholic kids went to a different school. Or why some kids got invited to Cotillion over others. It was just the way things were. So why ask why? No one else did; at least, not openly.

On the surface, people in my hometown were a "go along to get along" bunch. But scrape the surface and there were definite boundaries we all knew not to cross. Although my parents raised me with the noble Kipling adage, "Walk with Kings...nor lose the common touch,"[1] subliminally, by junior high, I understood this to mean to "keep the common touch but make sure the 'common' didn't touch me." So I never dated black boys. Jewish, Greek or Catholic either. Nor did any of them ask me out. Their parents no more wanted their sons getting serious about a white Protestant girl than mine wanted me getting serious with someone outside my own "culture." The message was

---

[1] From the poem, *If*, by Rudyard Kipling

clear: friends, fine, but at the end of the day, stick with your own kind. All our parents (mine less than most, actually) sang the same out-of-key tune: "Think about your future, and the future of your children…" Here all us teens wanted was a date and our folks kept making baby plans! Geez.

By the mid-1960s, the Civil Rights movement had heated up and the government pushed the schools to integrate. People resisted. Things got ugly. Bomb scares and threats of rioting reverberated across the nation. I was to be a member of the first white class to integrate the black high school in town. Mother, fearing danger, insisted I attend a local private school instead. But I was determined to stay the course, not as a statement of solidarity for integration so much, but because I'd always yearned to become a cheerleader at a big public high school

A year later, in 1968, Martin Luther King and Bobby Kennedy were assassinated. Tensions ran high. Hostilities between the races intensified. Los Angeles' Watts district and Washington, D.C.'s 14th Street corridor incinerated and burned to the ground. Crossing borders could have severe repercussions. I knew better than to tell my parents about sneaking off with other cheerleaders to black parties where the jokes were funny, the food tasty, the music soulful and the dancing, especially the slow dancing, out of this world. Then again, my parents were reasonable, loving people and I suspected I could risk an occasional night of fun with friends whose skin pigment was a few shades darker than mine. I just needed to be discreet.

Still, even after 18 months of college and a photography internship in Harlem, I remained disinterested in the politics of race, wealth and social class. Then I went to Jamaica where blatant economic, social and racial inequities exploded in my face. It was spring break of sophomore year. I'd saved my pennies and flown to visit a dorm mate at her family's vacation retreat in Runaway Bay. It was my first trip overseas, my first time in a different culture and my first taste of being a racial minority (which always lends a clarity to things).

Jamaica was a magnificent rush of high mountains, lush jungles and blinding white beaches set in a sapphire blue Caribbean sea. My friend's family lived in a community of big, white houses with pools, set high on a hillside overlooking the ocean. We spent the first few days relaxing poolside, sunbathing and swimming, followed by evenings of bridge and delicious meals prepared by the Jamaican housemaids. I wasn't particularly anxious to leave the luxurious compound and when I came down with a fever from sun-poisoning, I didn't mind being left behind while the others went out touring. I lounged in bed reading or puttered back and forth to the kitchen to sample island fruits the maids gave me. They were a jovial duo and the sing-song inflections in their accents delighted me. "You know, mahm, you eat da banana. Da banana a good ting. Heal da body, sure nuff now."

The next day, fever-free, my hosts took me on a shopping trip to the waterfront town of Ocho Rios where we spent several hours wandering through fancy shops. I noted that most of the storeowners and clerks were East Indian or Asian while most of the people sitting outside by decrepit, tin-roofed shanties were black. As we walked from store to store, I passed Jamaican women fanning themselves in shanty doorways, watching their young children happily splash in the shallow ocean water. Dark-skinned men in raggedy clothes sat nearby, smoking fat *ganja*[2] (marijuana) cigarettes, their long, unkempt mops of twisted hair streaming over their faces.[3] These Rastafarians were the strangest-looking people I'd ever seen and their bloodshot eyes and dull, distant stares—even though they bore no malice—unnerved me.

My hosts assured me that Rastas were a peaceful lot who stood for black pride, spirituality and anti-materialism. But the material disparities between the life these Jamaicans led and the lifestyles of the people up the hill bothered me. Did it bother my hosts, too, or the other people living in posh homes, running swank shops or managing fancy hotels? Or were they so used to the way of life there that they simply thought these people did not expect more for themselves? Familiarity has a curious way of blurring or even distorting reality. Then again maybe they wore the same blinders that I did at home and just accepted Jamaica's class structure as status quo. After all, "not seeing" makes life so much easier.

But in Jamaica, I saw only too well. The raw kind of seeing that comes with first sightings and fresh eyes. And the things I saw were difficult to ignore. The great chasms between rich and poor and black and white made me uncomfortable, and my instincts told me that being in a place where so few had so much and so many had so little was a potentially explosive situation.

That night, while the others played cards, I leafed through a book about Jamaica's fascinating, complicated history. It had it all. The original "Greatest Show on Earth." Buccaneers, privateers, pirates, Spanish galleon ships. Colonialism, slavery, indentured servitude, sugar. First plundered and ruled by the Spanish, then by the British, who wrangled control of it in the mid-1600s. For the next 300 years, British government coffers swelled and English nobility, merchants and plantation owners grew wealthy off the profits from sugar plantations cultivated by slave labor.

2   Rastafarians regard marijuana as a sacrament and use it to aid them in meditation.
3   The twisted coils of hair on Rastafarians, called *dreadlocks*, are grown to exemplify the image of the lion of Judah.

An age-old theme that left the pretty Caribbean island continually buffeted and battered by *wind wakes*: turbulent, forceful, mighty winds that are often produced around islands. Wind wakes benefit beachcombers because they generate large waves and strong winds that blow top layers of sand away, thus exposing hidden treasure. But the human backwash resulting from Jamaica's wind wakes was a sorry legacy of the few flourishing off the sweat of the many.

I continued to contemplate this history the next morning at Dunn's River Falls where we climbed up and lay on slippery river rocks, shivering as cool mountain waters rushed over our hot, sweaty bodies. From there we swam in aquamarine waters at white sand beaches, the sand so fine it coated my feet and ankles like socks. But aside from the occasional trinket seller, I had no interaction with Jamaicans. This went on for several days until finally, one morning, I grabbed my courage and my camera and, with my friend's older sister, accompanied the maids on a grocery run to Browns Town, an interior mountain town with a busy marketplace. We boarded a local bus overflowing with people and, as we moved along the misty rolling country-side, smells of wet leaves, damp turned earth and fragrant flowers wafted in through the open windows. The farther inland I traveled, the further removed I felt from the artificiality of seaside tourist haunts, four-star hotels and duty-free stores.

Browns Town was charming with old buildings and a large outdoor market where throngs of gaily-dressed people hovered around bountiful produce stalls, laughing, cajoling and shouting over each other as they bargained for food. I was one of a handful of white people in a sea of black faces—a somewhat unnerving situation—but everyone was so friendly and there was so much to take in, that my self-consciousness slipped away. As we wove through the crowd, I snapped pictures of the maids chatting with friends; of children mugging; of artful displays of plantains, papayas, watermelons and limes.

The market at Browns Town was as refreshing as the tourist town of Ocho Rios was stultifying. Walking through that buoyant crowd of strangers, I'd never experienced such uninhibited exuberance or felt more connected to the human race. I realized that if I hadn't accompanied the maids that day, I would never have seen the joyous side of Jamaican life or felt their incomparable zest for living. These people might have a poverty of things, I thought, but not a poverty of the spirit. A good lesson for one to learn who hailed from a society marked by materialism and always, always, the unquenched thirst for more.

I spent my last day of vacation swimming at Cardiff Hall, a public beach near Runaway Bay.

After a snorkel and a snooze, I moseyed along the shore 'combing for treasures. There wasn't much really. A few sticks of driftwood. A bit of coral. A bleached sea urchin or two. Then I came across a jagged-edged piece of pottery. It had a blue maker's mark of two lions encircling a crown with the words "Royal Ironstone China" printed beneath them. How fitting. A piece of British china. An emblem of centuries of colonial rule. Broken at last.

That pottery fragment marked the start of a life-long love of sea-tossed ceramics. That trip to Jamaica left me with another lasting legacy as well: it ripped the blinders off my eyes. When I returned home, I made more of an effort to cross borders. Step off the beaten track. Try new things. Travel more. Get to know people from other cultures or even just associate with more people outside my personal network.

Much like meeting up with fellow beachcombers or even strangers on a beach, crossing borders takes me to neutral places and easier spaces; where people approach each other on an equal footing and there is no jockeying for position or games of one-upmanship. Just good will and laughter and interesting stories to listen to and tell. Rastafarian prophet and reggae master Bob Marley[4] sang about this kind of emotional liberation all the time. "One love. One heart. Let's get together and feel alright." Jamaica introduced me to his beat and slowly, over the years, I have learned how to dance to it, even when I'm not on a beach.

---

[4] *One Love*, by Bob Marley

The Consummate Beachcomber

Jamaica

Totaling 4,244 square miles, Jamaica is one of the largest islands in the Caribbean. Its complex history of warfare, slavery, colonialism, a thriving plantation-based economy and tourism has few rivals in the region. The first known inhabitants of Jamaica were the Tainos, an Arawak-speaking Indian tribe from South America. Traveling widely throughout the Caribbean, they settled in Jamaica around 650 CE and named the island *Xaymaca* (Arawak for "Land of Wood and Water"). Spanish explorers later substituted J for the letter X.

Unlike other more war-like Carib tribes, the Tainos were peaceful farmers and fishermen who are credited with creating the hammock. Their peaceful way of life came to an abrupt halt, however, with the 1493 arrival of Spanish-funded, Italian explorer Christopher Columbus. Within two decades, the Spanish established a settlement and began enslaving the Tainos. By the 1660s, the Indian population was wiped out by European disease, suicide or hard slave labor so the Spanish then began importing captured Africans to replace the Tainos slaves.

Beginning in 1596, in an attempt to capture Jamaica for the Crown, the British launched periodic attacks on the Spanish. In 1655 the Spanish finally fled to Cuba, freeing and arming the slaves they left behind. These armed slaves formed a resistance group called the *Maroons* (still in existence), who set up camps in the island's interior and continued to conduct guerrilla warfare against the British, sometimes quite successfully. Meanwhile, to encourage more settlers, England offered grants of land to any of its citizens willing to relocate to Jamaica. Many jumped at the opportunity and, soon, vast sugarcane plantations peppered the island and Jamaica's economy boomed as it evolved into the world's largest sugar producer. Maintaining this caliber of economic power, however, required the importation of more and more African slaves, who subsequently were treated so poorly that Jamaica claimed the highest percentage of slave revolts in the West Indies.

In an attempt to ease tensions with the slave populations, the government granted *mulattoes* (racially-mixed people) access to political power in 1830. But it was too little a move done too late. In the 1831 Christmas Rebellion, 20,000 slaves rose up and killed scores of planters and destroyed thousands of acres of cash crops.[1] In response, landowners promised to abolish slavery if the slaves laid down their arms. When the slaves acquiesced, 400 of them were hung and many more whipped. Then, in 1834, the government passed an Emancipation Act, freeing slaves under age six and allowing all other slaves to apprentice in new work-related skills. Still in need of labor to turn out their cash crops, desperate planters began importing indentured servants from India and, later, China.

All of these political dramas were set against a backdrop of privateerism and piracy,[2] the likes of which the world had never before seen. From the late 1500s through the late 1700s, famous pirates such as renegade privateer-turned-pirate, Henry Jennings, and the nasty Blackbeard (Edward Teach) were scourges of the West Indies. A violent, lawless lot, they targeted Spanish armadas loaded with South American gold as well as European merchant ships delivering goods between the colonies, European markets and wealthy Jamaican planters. Calico Jack (Captain Jack Rackham), a particularly notorious pirate, was finally captured and hung in Jamaica in 1720.

[1] By the late 1830s, sugar's shifting fortunes led planters to turn to other cash crops (coffee, cocoa, bananas).

[2] *Privateers* were pirate sailors whose actions were sanctioned by nations. To gain a foothold in the Caribbean during the 16th and 17th centuries, France, England and the Netherlands used privately-owned ships to fight their battles with the Spanish. Privateers harassed the Spanish, disrupted trade, and even raided and burned their ships, splitting the plunder with the countries that commissioned them. *Pirates*, on the other hand, were ruthless lawbreakers, beholden to no one but themselves and their own codes of conduct. From a notorious base camp in Nassau, Bahamas, they roamed the Caribbean, robbing vessels and dividing the captured loot equally amongst themselves.

The 20th century proved to be a watershed in Jamaican history. Black Jamaican publisher and journalist Marcus Garvey began a worldwide campaign to encourage black nationalism. To aid in the effort, he founded Jamaica's first modern political party, the Peoples Political Party, in 1929. Over the next three decades, civil unrest diminished, unions were formed and tourism eclipsed agriculture as the island's leading income generator. In 1962 Jamaica gained independence from the British but remained a member of the Commonwealth of States. It was around this time that a religious/political movement known as Rastafarianism took hold. The movement, which grew out of Jamaica's violent history of slavery, recognized Africa as the birthplace of mankind. Rooted in the teachings of Marcus Garvey, Rastafarianism encouraged self-reliance and denounced both colonialism and the Eurocentric views that fostered shame amongst black people for their African ancestry. To this day, Rastafarians remain a proud, peaceful people who shun materialism and greed.

Ceramics

Unlike the gulf coast of Florida or other Caribbean islands, Jamaica is not a paradise for shell-seeking beachcombers. Most shells are found by snorkeling the reefs, where they serve as homes protecting living animals. On the beaches you may come across other interesting items, however, including driftwood, sea biscuits, sea urchins, some sand dollars and sea worms as well as the occasional piece of sea glass or ceramic shard. Ceramics include any item made of fired clay and can be differentiated in terms of composition, type of glaze, color, design and maker's mark. For the beachcomber, these characteristics can yield sufficient clues to determine a shard's origin, purpose and/or age.

There are three main categories of ceramics: pottery, stoneware and porcelain. Pottery is made from earthenware that is porous, coarse and easily breakable. It comes in brown, buff or off-white colored clay and is glazed to prevent moisture from seeping in. Stoneware ceramics, whose origins can be traced back to 500 BCE in China, are made from hard, dense clays that, when fired at very high temperatures, meld together to create an opaque, nonporous surface. Harder, denser, more durable and more water-resistant than earthenware, stoneware can be made into very thin pottery that artisans can decorate with elaborate molded or applied designs. In the 17th and 18th centuries, salt-glazed stoneware jars, jugs and crockery were popular in both European and American households because they were non-porous and able to keep things cool for extended periods. In the 1800s blue and gray stoneware were popular in colonial America as were tan-colored stoneware bottles.

The third category of ceramics, porcelain, is a name given to any hard, white, translucent ceramic. There are three types of porcelain: hard-paste porcelain, soft-paste porcelain and bone china. Hard-paste porcelain is hard, glassy, smooth and cold to the touch with a durable, shiny glass-like glaze. The Chinese began producing this porcelain in the Tang Dynasty (618-907 CE) by mixing and melting two ingredients together: *kaolin*, a pure white, clay-like substance highly resistant to heat, and *petunste*, a mineral found only in China. When heated to very high temperatures, these ingredients fuse to create a light, translucent ceramic. Other cultures tried for centuries to replicate this recipe with little luck. The Koreans finally succeeded in the 11th century, the Japanese in the 15th and the Europeans in the 18th.

Before the European discovery of the Chinese hard-paste porcelain formula, wealthy Americans and Europeans imported coveted "Chinese export" china to grace their dinner tables. Shards from these can sometimes be found on beaches located near early colonial settlements or on shores proximate to historic shipwrecks. More common finds are fragments of earthenware, stoneware, and 19th- and 20th-century hard-porcelain china by Japanese *Noritake*, French *Limoges* and American *Haviland* and *Lenox*.

Before a German potter stumbled on the hard-paste porcelain formula, Europeans relied on a soft-paste porcelain that combined ground glass stiffened with white clay. When fired at low temperatures this mixture created granular, porous, translucent china. Then in the early 19th century, Josiah Spode developed a hybrid, hard-paste porcelain ceramic he called bone china. By mixing animal bones with kaolin and petunste, Spode created a less expensive but reliable version combining aspects from both hard-paste and soft-paste porcelain. It is still the standard formula manufacturers use today.

Glazes are applied to ceramics to make the clay beautiful, watertight and smooth to the touch. Oftentimes, glazes can provide clues to the age, type or origin of ceramic shards found on the beach. Glazes on hard-paste porcelain are usually fused directly into the porcelain. Soft-paste porcelain pieces tend to have thicker glazes that do not fuse into the body. They may also have stains or dirt on the unglazed portions around their base, which don't disappear with cleaning. Stoneware was usually salt glazed which turned the ceramic an orangey color. Lead glazing, a common early form of pottery glazing, created a shiny, transparent appearance on the ceramic. So check to see if the glaze is shiny, dull, matte, thick, thin or grainy. The glaze on older pieces may have cracks or *crazing* (fine networks of lines) that can be discolored brown or gray from water or mud leaching into the ceramic.

Decorations, colors, designs and maker's marks also offer beachcombers excellent clues to determine a shard's origins or age. Designs can be molded, incised, printed, hand-painted, transferred or stamped. Blue was a commonly-used design color in American and English ceramics between the 17th and early 20th centuries. Maker's marks (on the underside of ceramics) can be embossed, stamped or painted. These marks offer excellent clues about a ceramic shard's manufacturer, date, quality, age and place of production.

The shard of Royal Ironstone china I found that day on the beach in Jamaica had a hallmark of *Johnson Brothers* on it, a china manufacturing firm in England. It was probably a fragment of ceramic made around 1880.

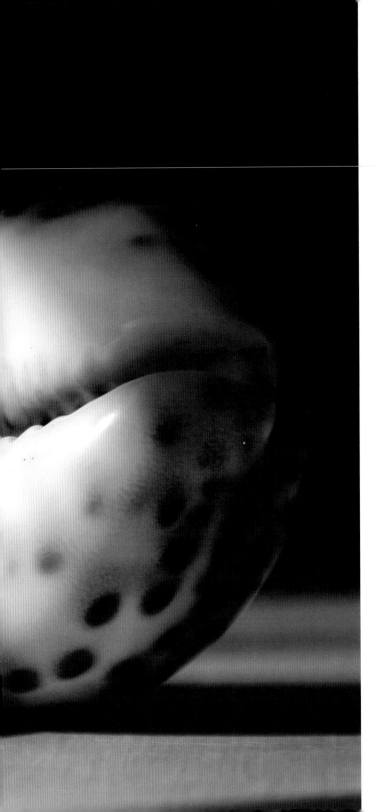

Chapter 9
Tidal Wave

*When there's nothing left
to lose, take a risk.*

*Winsome, spotted tiger cowries from the
Manu'a Islands in American Samoa*

Ta'u, American Samoa: *Tidal Wave*

"When there's nothing left to lose, take a risk."

One of my favorite childhood toys was a marionette named Heinrich. Heinrich wore a green hat and gray lederhosen and had strings attached to his hat and his pelvis. If I pulled his strings, he flapped his arms and legs up and down. If I pulled his strings very quickly, Heinrich danced. Sometimes I'd take Heinrich on family car trips where I'd sit in the back seat yanking the strings so fast that he danced in time to the radio music. This made everybody laugh. But one time when I yanked the strings, Heinrich's limbs lifted, then slumped into a lifeless heap. A frayed string had snapped. Heinrich was broken. He wouldn't be dancing for me any more.

There have been times in my life when I've felt as unstrung as Heinrich. The summer I was 19 and my beau of two years casually announced that he could live without me, then strolled off alone into the sunset was one. His good-bye confused me. He'd seemed so in love the week before. Wasn't being in love a permanent condition? Such a foolish, naive notion, I know. But then, I'd yet to experience the callousness that comes with a cooling ardor.

The demise of that relationship left me broken-hearted. It also turned my pat little game plan of early marriage, chubby babies and pleasant holidays at the shore upside down. For the rest of the summer, I kept to myself. Pretending things were fine took too much effort. Even the academic rigors and social activities of college that fall did little to lift my mood.

Then, one bleak November day, something snapped. I called my parents and announced that I was using an inheritance from my grandmother to move to Europe. Horrified that their youngest child and only daughter was moving to a place where they didn't know a soul, my parents talked me into flying to the South Pacific, instead, to stay with a brother employed there. Okay, I said. Why not? I didn't care where I went. I just wanted to get the hell out of Dodge. After I hung up, I promptly called a travel agent and booked a round-trip plane ticket to someplace called Pago Pago, American Samoa.

When you have nothing left to lose, you take a small sum of money and turn it into a great big risk.

So I waved good-bye to a cozy home and a complex family, to college texts and a lousy ex-boyfriend who could live without me, and jetted off to places unknown hoping that I, too, could learn to live without him. Even though I'd only been on a plane twice and had never traveled alone; even though the trip involved three stopovers, two plane changes, 18 hours of pressurized cabins and seven more of waiting in airports by myself; even with all those strikes against going, I didn't care. My life was such a dead zone, anything was better than what I had now. So what if the plane crashed, or a shark ate me, or I was kidnapped by restless natives? I needed fresh air, a new view, a clean slate; something, *anything* different to write home about. Perhaps in this strategy of spatial withdrawal I would rediscover my happier, more carefree self again. Twenty-four hours later the plane touched down on the steamy tarmac of the volcanic Samoan island, Tutuila. My experiment in international living was about to begin.

It was only meant to be a four-month sojourn during which I'd be safely ensconced in my brother's home. But within 72 hours he moved me to the home of a Samoan ex-girlfriend because, well, three's a crowd when you're caught up in a new affair. So there I was, alone again, this time in a strange country and an even stranger culture.

I never really fit into the scheme of things on Tutuila, though its languid beauty was inescapable. From the sky, the island resembled a mythical dragon writhing in a tumultuous sea. Sometimes I'd just sit, mesmerized by the magic of heavy mists or torrential rains moving across the dense green mountainsides. Often times I wandered through lush hotel gardens, where the humid air was thick with the sweet smell of plumeria, and the dance floor was always full of sultry, butter-skinned women swaying in time to slow-moving melodies. The island's *fa'afafines* (drag queens) were another treat altogether. Shaved, coiffed and more stylish than most local women, they sometimes used me as bait to lure unsuspecting sailors or male tourists into having a drink, a dance and maybe something more later. And it was while climbing down a cliffside, watching sinewy trails of smoke travel up from a remote coastal village, that the idea of becoming an anthropologist took hold.

But American Samoa also had a dark side, too; one that marred its loveliness. The sad truth was that it was little more than a welfare state, filled with restless, resentful repatriated Samoans, U.S. government personnel and assorted yachties. In the darkness of the Bamboo Room Bar, at any time of day, I'd hear people grousing about straying spouses or meager paychecks, their beer bottles forming ever-growing circles of sweat on black Formica tabletops. They seemed to have so many problems, mine paled in comparison.

Sometimes, after work, if I didn't time it right and get indoors before *Sa* (evening prayers), annoyed Samoan elders hurled rocks and insults at me as I scrambled up the rocky path to my Fagatogo home. Sometimes, too, screams from late night brawls in bar joints below drowned out the lovely strains of Korean music carried by trade winds from fishing boats across the harbor. And then there were the toads. Scores of them. Huge, passive, dull creatures that remained motionless blobs on the sidewalks or lay splattered on the tarmac in the middle of roads.

From habit, I turned to the shore for comfort. But, while most of Tutuila's beaches were beautiful to look at, they were also narrow or rocky, and usually hosted only broken chips of coral or dull, over-bleached cowry shells. I learned that the exquisite shells on display like prized trophies in many expatriate homes had first required the killing and extracting of the sea creatures inhabiting them. And these people called themselves nature lovers? Sheesh.

If Tutuila marked such a miserable period in my life, why didn't I pack up and return home after four months as planned? What kept me there? Was it pride? Stubbornness? Inertia? Or was it simply the belief that American Samoa was the best option I had while I waited for that letter from the ex-boyfriend begging me to come home?

Well, thank God for letters that never come. For if I hadn't extended my stay on Tutuila, I would never have visited Ta'u Island, a fortuitous interlude that changed the course of my life forever.

One of three postcard-perfect islands in American Samoa's isolated Manu'a group, the beauty of Ta'u was legendary. So, when a group of Samoan teachers invited me to join them on a holiday there, I jumped at the chance to tag along. Never having roamed the high seas of the Pacific before, I boarded the ferry the morning of departure with a mix of excitement and curiosity. The first leg of the overnight trip was filled with laughter, guitar music, singing and high spirits. By nightfall, however, a violent storm moved in and with it came unruly 15-foot swells that smashed into the bow of the boat. The drenched deck soon became a horrific vision of limp bodies periodically heaving overboard then slumping down exhaustedly onto the wet, filthy deck. One by one, my seasick friends disappeared, either shifting to the side rails or slinking off to out-of-the-way corners where they curled into silent, miserable, unmoving balls of flesh.

By midnight there was only one person left upright on deck—me—a wet, forlorn figure fighting nausea as noxious fumes spewed from the ferry's diesel engine. Finally, to escape the fumes, I skidded through the slippery darkness to the top deck where I crouched by a lifeboat, low enough to escape the salt spray, and started chain smoking in an effort to stay calm. Moments later, a tall, lanky figure appeared at the top of the stairs and, spotting me, headed my way. He bent down and asked for a cigarette then settled beside me to smoke it. He was an American from California, younger than I, on his way to Manu'a to visit a Samoan friend. He was already well traveled, and full of interesting stories and uncommon insights, and we sat with our backs pressed against the lifeboat, sharing cigarettes and talking above the wind. Though I can't recall much of it now, I remember thinking it was the best conversation I'd ever had in my life.

Dawn brought a calm ocean and serene blue sky. My new friend and I shared an orange and a bag of chips and watched as three small islands gradually rose on the horizon. Manu'a. Finally. Such romantic islands. The stuff of castaway legends. Buff-colored and emerald green with long, empty beaches and tiny villages of thatch-roofed *fales* (houses).[1] When we reached Ta'u, the ferry anchored beyond the reef as brawny Polynesian men in ripped jeans or vibrant *lava-lavas* (wrap-around loin cloths) rowed longboats out to transport us to shore.

The following morning my ferry friend arrived straddling an old, sputtering motorbike. We explored the island, cruising back and forth over the few miles of gravel road separating villages. Later that day and for the following week, I swam and played beach tag with village children, left messages in bottles, tried to climb coconut trees, snorkeled the reef and spied on *kava* ceremonies.[2] I even won a live chicken in a village dance contest! I knew I couldn't take the chicken home with me, but I could take two spotted cowry shells I'd found peeking out of the sand, each speckled with "brown sugar" freckles like the kind sprinkled across my face when I was a kid.

That week on Ta'u made me feel like a kid again, in the best sense of the word. Curious. Spontaneous. Caught up in the moment. It was as if I'd returned home from a long trip and found my old self waiting to greet me. I knew then that Samoa marked, not the end of the line for me, but the beginning. I knew, too, that it was time for this voyager to move on. Not back home, necessarily, but perhaps, "fair forward,"[3] to different worlds and new adventures. As I

[1] Traditional Samoan *fales* are oval, open-air style dwellings with woven fiber louvers that can be lowered at night to keep out wind, rain or "wandering minstrels."

[2] *Kava* is a root that many Pacific islanders pound into a powder, mix with water, strain and drink to enhance relaxation. In some countries kava is drunk only by men during ceremonial occasions (Samoa). In other countries kava is both a ceremonial and a social drink (Tonga, Fiji and Vanuatu). Village men often form kava clubs, where they come to share a cup of "grog," play music, socialize and discuss village affairs.

[3] Excerpted from T. S. Eliot's poem, *Dry Salvages*, section 3 of 5, when Krishna admonishes Arjuna on the field of battle.

packed for the return ferry trip to Tutuila, I resolved to leave American Samoa as soon as I could afford to and tucked the brown sugar cowries in my duffel to remind me of my resolve. I never saw or heard from my ferry friend again. Like an angel, he'd come into my life for only the briefest moment but his influence has had a lasting impact on me.

A few months later, using money I'd earned as a photographer, I purchased a round-trip plane ticket to New Zealand via Western Samoa, Tonga and Fiji. Over the next couple of years, I visited many islands and befriended people from all ethnicities and walks of life. When I finally returned stateside, brown as a berry with clothing patched and faded, I not only had interesting tales to tell (not that many wanted to hear them) but also a profoundly altered world view.

My brown sugar cowries take me back to that time when a broken heart propelled me toward taking the kind of risks that can be life changing. I hadn't been looking for answers in this strategic withdrawal. I just wanted to escape my situation. But the breathing space gained from that Pacific sojourn restored my equilibrium. It also taught me that, in the immortal words of cardsharp Lucas Jackson (*Cool Hand Luke*), "sometimes nothin' can be a real cool hand."[4]

4   As spoken by Paul Newman in the film *Cool Hand Luke*, novel by Donn Pearce, screenplay by Donn Pearce and Frank Pierson.

The Consummate Beachcomber

American Samoa
American Samoa, located in central Polynesia,[1] is about 2,600 miles south of Hawaii. A U.S. Territory, it comprises three eastern Samoan islands (Tutuila, Anu'u and Rose); three islands in the Manu'a group (Ta'u, Olosega and Ofu) and Swains Island. The territory's total land area is 77 square miles. Its largest island, Tutuila, is home to the nation's capital, Pago Pago (pronounced Pongo Pongo), as well as the South Pacific's finest mountain-protected, deep sea harbor. Formed from the remains of extinct volcanoes, Tutuila and the islands comprising the Manu'a group are rocky with tropical rainforests and prominent central mountain ranges.[2] Cone-shaped Ta'u, the largest island in Manu'a, also has the highest peak in the territory, Lata Mountain, which rises to more than 3,000 feet.

Current archaeological evidence suggests that American Samoa was settled around 600 BCE by Polynesian wayfarers arriving from Tonga and Western Samoa, probably via Indonesia, Vanuatu and Fiji. The

1   The islands of the western Pacific are divided into three groups: *Micronesia* (small islands), *Melanesia* (dark islands) and *Polynesia* (many islands).
2   The highest peak, Mt. Matafao on Tutuila, is 2,140 feet high. The most famous mountain, Mt. Pioa, is known as *The Rainmaker* because of its frequent cloud cover.

islands remained largely isolated from the European world until Jacob Roggeveen, a Dutch explorer, sighted the Manu'a group in 1722. A little more than 100 years later, in 1831, Englishman John Williams arrived with eight Tahitian Christian missionaries. Samoans embraced this new religion with an enthusiasm that continues today.

As part of an agreement between Germany, England and the U.S., American Samoa (with the exception of Swains Island) became a U.S. territory in 1900. The U.S. operated a naval base in Pago Pago until World War II during which time the islands became an important staging area for the U.S. Marines in the Pacific Theater. After the war, the territory settled back into quiet obscurity and Samoans continued to practice a *fa'a Samoa* (traditional) way of life revolving around the *aiga* (extended family) and subsistence farming and fishing.

The push to modernize the country began in the 1960s when the territorial constitution was ratified, turning American Samoa into a self-governing political system with elected officials. The U.S. government then began pumping development money into the country, updating its infrastructure and information delivery systems. Over the next several decades, as the territory became more and more dependent on loans and grants from the U.S. government, the self-sufficient Samoan lifestyle, at least on Tutuila, largely disappeared.

Cowry Shells

American Samoa's warm water and extensive coral reef system offers a desirable home for many exotic mollusk and fish species, including sea anemone and coral; the gaudily-colored lion fish, clown fish and parrot fish; and beautiful shells such as olive, auger and cowry shells. Cowries, in particular, are much sought after for their smooth and highly polished shells. Of the *Cypraeidae* family, cowries are univalve gastropods that live in tropical and semi-tropical waters worldwide. They hide under rocks by day and feed on algae at night. Like other gastropods, cowries have a distinct head, with tentacles and a radula. They also have a beautiful orange mantle that wraps around the entire shell, protecting its surface and camouflaging it from predators. The cowry's smooth, shiny, egg-shaped shell—called *porculi* (little pigs) by the early Romans—sets it apart from other univalves, for as the shell develops, its growing edge eventually thickens, turns inward and forms *teeth* (ridges) along either side of the aperture.

In many societies, the cowry shell is believed to bring good luck and offer protection from the "evil eye." Cowries have been used as items of trade for thousands of years in Africa, Asia and the South Seas. In some Pacific island cultures, especially those in Melanesia, cowries were—and in some places, still are—regarded as wealth and are often used in the exchange of goods, as part of a bride's dowry or to signify status. Some cultures use cowries as decorations on clothing, hats, mats and fans., while others transform them into octopus lures or attach them to fishing nets. There are currently more than 250 known warm-water species of cowry. The tiger cowry—like those I found on Ta'u—are some of the most common. The rare golden cowry, on the other hand, found in the cracks and crevices of South Pacific reefs, is one of the most sought-after shells in the world.

Chapter 10
Spindrift

The secret to patience is finding something else to do.

The not-so-common chocolate-flamed Venus is an intriguing bivalve from the shores of Tonga.

Nuku'alofa, Kingdom of Tonga: *Spindrift*

The secret to patience is finding something else to do.

I have a large, round container inlaid with mother of pearl in which I store keepsakes. Little more than a crudely hollowed out tree trunk, it comes from the isolated Tokelau Islands in Central Polynesia, near Western Samoa. Originally intended as a bait box, mine holds funny notes from Dad, an origami sailboat, my hair braid shorn the summer I was 12 and the first present I ever purchased with my own money: a necklace with a rhinestone pendant for Mother from Murphy's Five and Dime.

At the bottom of this container is a small white cardboard box stained with age. Inside it are eight small clam shells and a note from me to Mother. I found the box the week after Mother died, in her bureau drawer buried under some lavender sachets. Funny, isn't it? Of all the exquisite things I sent to her from my travels, it was these seemingly unspectacular clam shells etched in haphazard brown calligraphy that she valued most.

What did these shells say to her, I wondered? What was the message hidden in their Morse code of dots and dashes? "Hi Mom. Having lots of fun but don't worry. I'll be home soon." Maybe, instead, she deciphered a deeper message in their designs; a more subliminal one. "She will return to you some day. For now, have patience. Let her learn how to breathe on her own."

Whatever the message, I hope it helped her bide her time because that trip to the Pacific drifted from months into years when I fell in love with a sleepy Polynesian Kingdom called Tonga. From the moment my plane landed in a tropical downpour, scattering pigs and chickens in its crazy skid across the runway, my heart was captured. All thoughts of returning home evaporated into thin air.

In the early 1970s Nuku'alofa, Tonga's capital city, reminded me of a 19th-century New England whaling village overlaid onto an 18th-century engraving from a Captain Cook expedition. Whitewashed cottages surrounded by hibiscus hedges intermingled with thatched huts and palm trees. There were no traffic lights, few streetlights and even fewer cars. People got around on foot, bicycle, horse-drawn cart, overcrowded bus or three-wheeled motorized taxis called *ve'etolu*. Tongans wearing somber-colored *tupenu* (tailored, wrap-around skirts) and traditional *ta'ovala* (traditional waist mats) idled on street corners laughing and talking, or ambled gracefully under umbrellas down dusty city streets to buy yams at the outdoor market.

There was an easygoing graciousness that came with living in Tonga back then, with a slow-as-molasses pace that could drive foreign newcomers wild. Yes, it could take hours to buy bread at Cowley's Bakery, retrieve mail at the post office or withdraw money from the Treasury. But somehow, everything always got done. On time, too. Or rather, on "island" time.

Each day, after teaching English at a local high school, I'd pass through town to my village, Ma'ofanga, where the view shifted from European-style bungalows on manicured lawns to more traditional oval-shaped huts adjacent to taro patches. My house, an unpainted, crudely built, one-room shack on stilts, sat in the midst of one such taro patch. It had no electricity or running water and only hinged boards to prop open for windows. My Samoan-American roommate and I christened it "Holey Hut" because the floorboards were so large that, during rainy season, we could watch ducks swimming in circles beneath us.

The hut was located two blocks from the ocean, so I'd often walk there after dinner to wait for the sun to set. Usually, I'd just sit on the seawall watching villagers scour the reef for *muli'one* (sea cucumber) as fishermen brought in the day's catch from dory to dock. The serene view of still water, silent slow-moving figures, tiny islands and soft pink sky reminded me of home, and I often felt I was in both places at once—my birth home and my adopted home—and it felt good.

Sometimes, if I grew impatient for the sunset, I'd scan the narrow shoreline for shells. But all I ever saw were clam shells that were so common everyone ignored them, so I did, too. Then, one day, feeling more impatient than usual, I decided to hop down from the seawall and collect a few. At least it was something to do until sunset. As I walked the beach collecting shells, I noticed that no two shared the exact same code-like design. Intrigued, I gathered more.

Over the next few months, I studied hundreds of clam shells but never found any with an identical pattern, not even on co-joined shells. The unlimited possibilities of shell patterning struck me as surreal. A remarkable natural wonder, like human fingerprints. Equally remarkable was how quickly the sun set when I kept busy collecting shells.

From age 20 to 38, my formative adult years, I lived in Tonga for extended periods of time. Subtle, slow-paced Tonga, resembling in so many ways the unspectacular clam shell on its shores, taught me a great deal about the quiet things in life, such as humility and simplicity. I also learned that some things can't be rushed but, instead, must be given time to unfold. This called for patience, never my strong suit. Being able to wait with grace did not come naturally. I had to learn it and earn it, slowly and steadily, day by day. Keeping busy with other things seemed to aid my efforts. And sometimes in the process I'd stumble on valuable lessons that could so easily have been overlooked. Like finding the extraordinary in the ordinary: the blessing of *spindrift* on a hot day, when fine, windblown sea spray slips in and cools a warm brow, or discovering that Tonga's common clam shells—the ones people so casually step on as they walk up the beach—are really not so common after all.

The Consummate Beachcomber

The Kingdom of Tonga

Tonga is a small Polynesian island kingdom situated in the central South Pacific just south of Western Samoa and east of Fiji. Located on the International Dateline, Tonga is often referred to as "the place where time begins." The country comprises 150 islands ranging from tiny coral atolls to raised islands to active volcanoes. Only 36 of these islands are inhabited.

Archaeological evidence[1] suggests that Tonga, along with Fiji and Western Samoa, was settled more than 3,000 years ago by voyaging seafarers moving in from the western Pacific. About 1,000 year later, these seafarers began fanning out across the Pacific, forming settlements in the Cook Islands, Tahiti, the Marquesas, New Zealand, Hawaii and Easter Island.

Long before European contact in the 1600s, Tongans developed an elaborate, highly-stratified society of chiefs, commoners and slaves. The Tu'i Tonga dynasty, from which the current King is descended, can be traced back to the late 9th century. Several large stone monuments, including the 12th-century Ha'amonga-a-Maui and the Royal Tombs, offer evidence of a strong political organization and a surplus of people.

The first Europeans to arrive in Tonga were the Dutch in 1616 who were looking for trade opportunities in the isolated northern Niua group. Later, in 1643, another Dutchman, explorer Abel

[1] Linguistic and material evidence sheds some light on the Tongan peoples place of origin. The discovery of a style of pottery, coined *Lapita*-ware after the place where it was first discovered, can be traced to New Caledonia in Melanesia. There are also systemic similarities in grammar and vocabulary between Melanesian and Polynesian languages.

Tasman, also spent time in Tonga before reaching New Zealand and, later, Tasmania, an island off Australia that was subsequently named for him. One hundred thirty years later, in 1773, legendary British explorer Captain James Cook arrived in time for the 'inasi (share) festival, a ceremony wherein the first fruits of the season were offered in tribute to the paramount chief. Cook described the islands as abundant with food and politically stable, and was so impressed with Tongan hospitality that he named the place The Friendly Islands. Unbeknownst to him, however, the "friendly" Tongan chiefs had actually been plotting to kill him, but couldn't agree on a plan.

Shortly after Cook's second visit in 1777, civil war broke out between the three chiefly lines. Conflicts did not abate until the 1830s. In the midst of these political upheavals, an odd mix of European settlers arrived, including escaped convicts from New South Wales and Christian missionaries from the London Missionary Society. Neither group had much influence on the Tongan people although subsequent missionaries did. Today Tonga has one of the highest percentages of practicing Christians in the world.

The current royal dynasty of Tonga was founded in 1831 by Taufa'ahau Tupou, who consolidated the Kingdom by conquest. In 1875 he transformed the government into a Constitutional Monarchy. Unlike the rest of the island nations in the Pacific, Tonga was never colonized by a colonial power. It did, however, become a British protectorate in 1900 but on July 4, 1970, gained its independence.

In the 1970s increasing population pressures on limited land resources resulted in extensive overseas migrations. In the last 30 years, the more sophisticated tastes of returning expatriots, the income generated from overseas remittances, and the clamor for greater democratic freedoms have made Tonga's quiet, subservient, subsistence lifestyle a thing of the past. This is especially true on the more westernized main island, Tongatapu, where Nuku'alofa is located. But many of Tonga's outer islands still maintain a distinctly traditional Polynesian ambiance.

Tongan Shells

The Tongan island chain has scores of islets and deserted sandy beaches to explore. Beachcombing there can be a very satisfying experience. Along with shells, 'combers will find sea glass, coral, glass floats and driftwood (sometimes made from eerie mangrove root). Significant barrier reefs rich in marine life surround some of the islands and are home to many exotic gastropods. Shells such as cones, volutes and olives can be found as well as the chocolate flamed Venus clamshell, which I collected on city beaches near Nuku'alofa.

Venus shells are bivalves and are some of the most intricately marked of all clam shells. They can be found along the shorelines or buried in the sand in warm and temperate waters worldwide. The chocolate flamed Venus shell is a white shell consisting of fine concentric lines that give its surface a smooth glossy appearance. Dark brown zigzags or hieroglyphic-style markings weave across the shell's surface in very bold and daring patterns.

Chapter 11
Flotsam and Jetsam

Periodically rake the beach.

A colorful plastic beach sailor who lost his head and his boat in some very stormy weather.

Gloucester, Massachusetts: *Flotsam and Jetsam*

Periodically rake the beach.

Gosh, there's a lot of trash on the beach! Has it always been this bad? Or am I only noticing it more? Are people getting lazier? Or is trash getting tougher to eradicate? Some days, weeks, even months, seem particularly overwhelming. The beaches become mired in mounds of rotting seaweed laced with plastic bottles, old sneakers, rubber toys and refuse having to do with contraception, injections or stemming blood. Ugh. What place does any of this have here? The answer, of course, is no place. So I get out the rake and do some beach cleaning.

This is how my life can be. Over time, the haphazard accumulation of things—papers, experiences, acquaintances—reaches a point where I am so weighed down I can barely move. Having so much clutter leaves little room for the real treasures that make life rewarding.

It is a continual battle, being a collector. What's worse, I then leave these collections in mounds all over the house. Mound building may be an inherited trait. I can't ever remember a life without clutter, even as a child. The clutter process begins with someone offering me something they no longer want. I usually take it, either because I could use it or I know someone who could. But then I never get around to putting it away or dropping it off. Soon, mounds of stuff grow to the point where we can't walk through the house without detouring around baskets overflowing with miscellany. Or, while looking through a magazine, I'll find an interesting article and tear it out. My office begins overflowing with clippings until finally, in a fit of pique, I'll spend days re-reading, sorting, tossing or filing articles that, in all likelihood, I never will refer to again.

The accumulation of negative emotions—grudges, hurts, resentments, hostilities—is equally crippling but much harder to toss away. Often, these emotions "talk trash" inside your head. The kind of talk that diminishes self-confidence and makes you question your judgment. Raking negative thoughts out of my psyche is hard work, but not impossible if I remain attentive and refuse to give in to it. Prayer helps, too. So does distraction.

The most dangerous accumulations throughout my life, however, involve relationships. I've found it difficult to disentangle from people. Bad relationships can't just be dropped off at Goodwill or put out with the trash. I learned this lesson when I moved from the South Pacific to Boston in 1974. Having lived among congenial Annapolitans and then with good-humored Polynesians, I was ill-equipped to deal with the level of neuroses I encountered in a big city like Boston. Moving there was like jumping from a garrulous but cozy Rosamunde Pilcher novel into a dry, tormented John Updike one. Forget the uptight, reserved New England manner, which would have been a relief. During that era of my life it seemed every other person I met was hyper-competitive or an authority of some kind; on drugs or recovering from them; in the midst of a divorce or "happily" married but having an affair with the nanny. If I showed little interest in specific social or political agendas, I was quickly dismissed for the next potential convert. I met unhappy people who cut themselves or tried to kill themselves or who drew sexually suggestive pictures on napkins over dinner. There was one particularly exhausting fellow who was always coming around. He talked a lot, his hands shook and his mouth was always dry. He scared me but I didn't have the heart to ignore him. I realize now he was probably taking medication for some mental illness, but back then I was clueless.

I knew there were lots of wonderful people in Boston. I saw them walking on the street, laughing with each other, their collars turned up against the cold, or having animated conversations in cafés or joking in lines outside movie theaters. They were out there. I just didn't know how to meet them.[1]

One wintry day a kindly Greek friend drove me to Good Harbor, my favorite swimming beach in Gloucester, on the beautiful Cape Ann peninsula. No one else was about, perhaps because the day was damp and very windy and the sky a gunmetal gray. It was low tide, so we were able to walk across the sandbar to Salt Island. The rocky shoreline was littered with broken bottles and rusted wire lobster traps mired in ominous slimy strands of kelp. The island felt lonely and forlorn, as if in need of love and attention.

We hunkered behind some boulders out of the wind's way to share a thermos of coffee and talk. I told him how unhappy I was and wondered why all the weirdos and angry people were attracted to me. Was there something in the air or was it the way I looked? Perhaps an invisible sign around my neck alerted them, "I'm a sucker. Please walk all over me. P.S. Thanks for the attention." My friend listened quietly and then said two profound sentences: "You attract these people because you listen to them. Cut it out."

---

[1]   Having grown up in a small town where I took knowing people for granted, it never occurred to me to join a club or do community or volunteer work as a way to meet people and make new friends.

These people are attracted to me because I listen to them? I was not a victim? I could actually *choose* whether or not to associate with these people? What a revelation!

After that conversation I began to see that people come with a fundamental energy: an up energy, a down energy, a calm or edgy energy, a generous or selfish one, healing or toxic. Even though my instincts about people are usually right on target, when I lived in Boston I ignored my cautionary inner voice because I found it fun to flirt, or was fascinated by danger, or thought someone needed saving, or I was just plain lonely. But I paid a price for these choices. I grew depressed. I began to experience panic attacks. For a while, I lost my way.

Just as the beauty of a beach can be overwhelmed by too much flotsam and jetsam, too much struggle and strangeness in life can leave one feeling bruised and battered. Nowadays, I listen to my instincts more and try to surround myself with life livers and givers. I tend to steer clear of people whose values and lifestyles leave me uncomfortable or whose conduct makes me feel grimy, ashamed or on edge.

Beachcombing teaches that we must follow the light to see more clearly, discard the unnecessary and pocket the best for safekeeping. In other words: keep it simple, be straightforward, deliberate and discriminating. These are the rakes we need to strike the chaff from our existence and remove the seaweedplasticgunk from our shores.

The Consummate Beachcomber

Gloucester on Cape Ann
Gloucester is America's oldest seaport with a historic maritime significance few others rival. Located about 30 miles northeast of Boston, Gloucester—along with the towns of Rockport, Manchester and Essex—is located on beautiful Cape[1] Ann.[2] The main part of the town, which transverses the Cape from one side to the other, is an island connected to the mainland by two bridges. American Indians of the Agawam tribe lived in this area prior to settlement by Europeans in the early 1600s. The first documented European sighting was in 1606 when Samuel de Champlain sailed into what is now Gloucester harbor, naming it *Le Beau Port* (beautiful port).

In 1623 a group of pilgrims[3] in search of good fishing grounds set up a temporary settlement and *fish*

---

[1]   A *cape* is a point of land projecting out into the ocean.
[2]   The cape of land was originally named by Prince Charles of Denmark after his mother, Anne.
[3]   These pilgrims were from the original colony that landed at Plymouth Rock in 1620.

stages (fish-drying platforms) in the area. Other immigrants arrived from England soon after. As the settlement grew, it was re-named Gloucester because so many of its inhabitants hailed from Gloucester, England. The settlement was incorporated in 1642 and, over the years, fish houses, wharves, boats and drying racks were built to accommodate the city's expanding maritime industries.

Gloucester is one of America's first true melting pots, populated by waves of different ethnic groups: Irish, Portuguese, Italian, Scandinavian, Nova Scotian. The toughness of Gloucester fishermen is legendary. In 1876 fisherman Alfred Johnson became the first person to sail solo across the Atlantic Ocean. Later, in 1883, Howard Blackburn became lost off the coast of Newfoundland and rowed for four days before reaching land, his hands frozen to the oars and his dead dory mate at his side. In 1991, the heartbreaking story of the sinking of the Gloucester fishing boat, the *Andrea Gail,* was immortalized in a book by Sebastian Junger, *The Perfect Storm,* which was later made into a movie.

Since the 1880s Gloucester has been a popular summer destination. Today, the city's annual seafood festival draws thousands and the town remains a pleasant place for a holiday or a day trip en route to the area's many fine public beaches including Good Harbor, Half Moon, Wingaercheek, Crane's at Ipswich and Plum Island Nature Preserve.

Beach Trash

Public consideration has paid off for Cape Ann's beaches and Gloucester's are some of the cleanest I have wandered in the last 20 years. I wish the same were true of Chesapeake Bay, the Jersey Shore, and other U.S. waterways, especially those adjacent to urban areas. Although I see fewer cigarette butts when beachcombing these days, there are still far too many plastic bottles and plastic toys, tangles of fishing line, deflated balloons and creepy-looking medical equipment.

During the summer of 1987 there was a 50-mile-long trail of trash that washed up on the shores of Ocean County, New Jersey. The garbage originated at a city incinerator and trash transfer station in Brooklyn and included hypodermic syringes and noninfectious waste from New York City hospitals.[4] Chesapeake Bay beaches suffer similar problems whenever the state of Pennsylvania opens floodgates of the Susquehanna River Dam. Within days, bay shorelines are littered with logs, rubber tires, industrial waste and other human-generated garbage. The problem of beach debris, however, is not endemic to east coast beaches but is a problem throughout the world.

In 1987 Congress passed Public Law 100-220, which includes the Marine Plastic Pollution Research and Control Act (MPPRCA). The objectives of this law are to try to control issues concerning plastic waste in the environment, including improper disposal of plastics from vessels, and to address the problem of humans littering on land. But littering is made worse because there are more and more people making more and more trash composed of materials—particularly plastics and nylons—that time and nature have difficulty breaking down. To ease the pollution problem, be like me. Go beachcombing. Throw away the trash you don't want and clutter up your house with the rest....

Chapter 12
Ebb Tide
Take time to re-align.

*Atlantic slipper shells from
Martha's Vineyard, lined up one by one*

Martha's Vineyard, Massachusetts: *Ebb Tide*

Take time to re-align.

The summer after that first difficult year in Boston, I went on holiday to Martha's Vineyard with my family. Still reeling from re-entry into fast-paced America from slow-paced Polynesia, I hoped a quiet holiday at the beach would do me good. Perhaps, to paraphrase Roethke, the lively understandable spirit that once entertained me would come again if I kept still and waited.[1]

We stayed in an inexpensive rental cottage on a back road near the fishing village of Menemsha. It had every amenity required for a pleasant beach vacation, including a deck facing the dunes and a quiet Vineyard Sound beach. But it was the even smaller shack next door that intrigued me, not because it was an impressive structure. It wasn't. It stood alone and abandoned on a windswept dune. Unadorned. Shingle-gray. Stoic. Each day, as I wandered along the beach below, I wondered why no one was there, sitting on the porch, enjoying the sunny summer weather, maybe even waving hello.

Ever curious, one day I just walked up and peeked in. The one-room interior was plain but inviting. Two rough-cut bunk beds were in one corner. A rudimentary kitchen was in the other. Except for a lumberjack coat that hung on a peg by the back door, there were no other signs of life. No crumbs on the counter, pots on the stove or sheets on the beds. Then my eyes settled on a table by the bay window. There, lined up from small to large, were pairs of slipper shells that someone, at some time, had gathered from the beach. They looked like wooden clogs expectantly awaiting little Dutch feet to step in and take them for a walk by the Zider Zee.

I'd collected a fair share of slipper shells myself on the beach that week. It wasn't difficult. They were everywhere. Single shells. Shells linked in chains or stacked one atop the other. Shells in clumps attached to rocks. Were slipper shells homebodies who enjoyed each other's company? Or scaredy cats, clinging to each other because there's safety in numbers? Maybe, like most of us, it was both. I particularly liked the large, wide-bottomed shells with colorful purple or brown interiors. They reminded me of the wooden boat that Winken, Blinken and Nod sailed away in.

[1] The precise quote from the poet Theodore Roethke is, "A lively understandable spirit once entertained you. It will come again. Be still. Wait."

Each day, for the remainder of the vacation, I'd sleep in, have a late breakfast, then head to the beach for a dip and some 'combing. I'd also spend a few hours by myself sitting in the sun on the porch of the shack, reading, writing or simply staring off into the endless horizon. Those hours were so peaceful, like "wide water, without sound,"[2] and the lifestyle the shack seemed to promise—singular, simple, uncluttered—greatly appealed to me. Being there was like living through a favorite poem a former student of mine had written:

> *And I would walk down sand and see*
> *Birds and think of simpler things*
> *And write it all down in my little black book*
> *And be pleased and continue to grow*
> *And simply have a good time, be peaceful,*
> *Feel cool and wet and comfortable and*
> *Have nothing, I know, waiting for me to do,*
> *Something I should do, whence I get back home.* [3]

Like an ebb tide, those quiet, reflective weeks on Menemsha allowed me to catch my breath. Looking back, I see that I was simply in the eye of a very big hurricane. Bad weather was behind me. Turbulent weather lay ahead. But, for now, my spirit sufficiently replenished, I felt I could face whatever new trials life washed up onto my shore, and when I boarded the ferry back to the mainland, I did so with a firmer step than when I arrived.

Though I have still not mastered the art of a balanced life, I have learned that I handle tumultuous times best if surrounded by gentle things: kind, patient people; soft lights; fresh flowers; a return to order; and walks on the beach. Beachcombing, in particular, is a saving grace during such interludes. Intently searching for a particular color of sea glass or type of shell provides me with a detached peacefulness that comes from focusing on something outside myself. If only for a short period of time, I am a child again with no history, no deadlines and no commitments. My only job is to seek out treasure, then sort, organize and glory in it. The smallness of my sights temporarily makes my world an easier place to bear, keeps me focused on the present moment, and helps me bide my time until the joyfulness of being returns. "Be

[2]   Written by a favorite poet of mine, Wallace Stevens
[3]   This untitled poem was written by my former student, Justin Doebele, when he was in the 11th grade. He is now a writer for Forbes Magazine.

unencumbered of what troubles you," Witter Bynner comforts. "Arise with grace and greatly go, the wind upon your face." [4]

Sometimes now when I lie on the sand, I'll close my eyes and let the rhythmic sound of waves lead me back to that dune shack on Menemsha. I picture myself sitting in the morning light by the bay window, doing simple, easy, straightforward things like lining up slipper shells, two by two, from small to large.

[4] *Grieve Not for the Beauty,* by Witter Bynner

The Consummate Beachcomber

Martha's Vineyard
Martha's Vineyard, the largest island on the southeastern coast of Massachusetts, is located six miles off the coast of Cape Cod. Some 20 miles long and nine miles wide, it is home to several charming towns including Oak Bluffs, Edgartown and Chilmark.

The earliest known inhabitants, the Wampanoag Indians, called the island *Noepe* (which means "In the Midst of the Sea"). The first Europeans to visit Martha's Vineyard may have been Vikings, or *Northmen*, who explored the region around 1000 CE. In 1524 the Italian explorer Verrazano sighted the island, but it was not until 1602, with the arrival of Englishman Bartholomew Gosnold,[1] that a first account was made. Gosnold found the island covered with woods and varied vegetation, with an array of beaches, lakes, pure springs, wild berries, and such an abundance of grape vines that he named it Martha's Vineyard after his infant daughter.[2]

In 1607 Captain Martin Pring anchored in what is now Edgartown harbor and built a stockade on Chappaquiddick Bluffs. Pring enjoyed trade with the Indians, amused them with music and took pleasure in terrifying them with canon fire and his pet Mastiffs. At the first sign of hostility from the Wampanoag, however, the 'brave' Captain Pring hightailed it out of there with a cargo of coveted sassafras root in his hold.

The first permanent European settlers arrived on Martha's Vineyard in 1642. By all accounts, relations between the Wampanoag and the settlers were cordial. But as the number of foreigners grew, the Indians shifted away from the growing European settlement to Gay Head on the island's western tip where

[1] Driven off course by contrary winds, Gosnold landed in the Azore Islands. From there he sailed a little north, then boldly headed west across the Atlantic to the New World. Gosnold's route saved nearly one thousand miles in distance and at least a week in sailing time, thus giving other European explorers a shorter and more direct route to America. Eighteen years later the Mayflower followed his route, landing in Plymouth, Massachusetts.

[2] Before reaching Martha's Vineyard, Gosnold landed on a nearby cape with such an abundance of cod fish that he christened it Cape Cod.

some Native Americans live to this day.[3]

Because of its location, sound harbors and fresh water, Martha's Vineyard was soon considered a place of importance on the newly-discovered American coast. In 1668 the islands of Martha's Vineyard, No-Man's-Land Island, Chappaquiddick[4] and the Elizabeth Islands were incorporated as Dukes County. The Vineyard became a major anchorage and, over the next 200 years, its economy prospered from farming, fishing and whaling. With the introduction of the locomotive and the discovery of fossil fuels, however, fortunes took a downward turn until the late 1800s. Then tourism took hold. Today Martha's Vineyard, with its charming villages, jagged cliffs and quiet ponds is such a favorite holiday haven that, like Nantucket, its population inflates to more than 100,000 each summer.

The town of Chilmark and its fishing port and harbor, Menemsha, are located on the Vineyard's quieter, less touristy west end. This area is marked by old stone walls, meadows filled with grazing sheep, fields of wildflowers and expansive views of the south shore. Because of its isolation and relative self-sufficiency, locals refer to this area as the "Independent State of Chilmark."

Menemsha (Wampanoag for "Still Waters") is located in the sheltered harbor of Vineyard Sound. Nearby, hugging the northwestern slope of the island's second-highest peak, is the 200-acre Menemsha Hills Reservation, which is open to the public for nature outings.

The Common Atlantic Slipper Shell

The common Atlantic slipper shell, also known as a *boat* or *quarterdeck* shell, is a favorite of shell seekers. Its resemblance to a bedroom slipper or a boat hull is due to a white partition—sometimes called the deck—that covers and splits the shell cavity in half. Slipper shells grow to about one to two inches long. Their outer surface can be either smooth or wrinkled and are commonly colored brown, maroon, white or any combination thereof.

This gastropod can be found from Canada to Texas and on the shores of northern Europe. It lives in shallow water in the intertidal zone between the high and low tide lines. After two years of drifting, the young molusks finally settle down and attach themselves to rocks or to each other for the remainder of their lives. It is not uncommon to find clumps or chains of slipper shells on the beach or in shallow water. But the fact that slipper shells form into groups has less to do with safety than it does with pragmatism: it makes reproduction easier and more efficient.

---

[3] Gay Head remains an Indian township, one of two such townships in Massachusetts. Unlike American Indians in most other areas in the country, Massachusetts Indians were not harshly dispossessed but received payment for their land.

[4] Wampanaoag for "Island off the Island."

Chapter 13
Strandlines

*The essence of life is change,
so keep a wider perspective;
today's setbacks are
tomorrow's dust in the wind.*

*A collection of prehistoric fossils
from the Miocene period,
all found at Calvert Cliffs, Maryland*

Calvert Cliffs, Maryland: *Strandlines*

The essence of life is change, so keep a wider perspective; today's setbacks are tomorrow's dust in the wind.

Wind and waves make beachcombing a productive pastime, so I am always a little disappointed when these elements are absent for any length of time. This happens most often in the summer when the air becomes heavy with humidity and the water becomes sluggish. A listless quality permeates the atmosphere, as if the world has stopped turning.

When I returned to Boston after my Menemsha holiday, my world stopped turning, too, and nothing I hoped for happened. A scholarship to complete college fell through. The roommate I'd planned to live with moved elsewhere. The internship I sought with a prestigious magazine never materialized. The momentum had evaporated from my life and I didn't know why. Everyone else my age seemed to have it all together (or maybe they were just better at faking it), but my life had stalled. Like the great sea level shifts that come with a *proxigean* tide,[1] I'd had great highs from traveling the world followed by real lows after my return home. Now I found myself as stuck as a shell on a strandline.

Strandlines are those places on the shore where things roll in with the waves at high tide and are abandoned. Strandlines may offer good pickings for birds and beachcombers but, emotionally, a strandline is a pretty gloomy place to be. You begin to believe that things will never change and, worse, that you are powerless to affect change. Like the Ancient Mariner[2] at sea, trapped in the doldrums with nary a breath of wind in sight, you wonder if you, too, will ever see land again.

The panic attacks I'd been experiencing since early spring intensified and nothing I did—yoga, brisk walks, cutting out caffeine—diminished them. Not knowing what else to do, I simply

---

[1] Ironically, the sun is closer to earth in winter than in summer, which increases its gravitational effects on the earth. This, in turn, makes tidal changes more dramatic. *Proxigean* tides can be so high that they overwhelm the shoreline one moment and then, six hours later, be so low that hundreds of feet of sea floor, normally underwater, are exposed. A proxigean low tide, especially if it comes after a bad storm or a strong wind, is one of the best times to go beachcombing.

[2] *The Rime of the Ancient Mariner* is an extended English poem written by Samuel Taylor Coleridge.

soldiered on but found myself increasingly confused and indecisive. Secretly I worried that I was going mad, and finally confided as much to my mother.

"You might be neurotic, honey, but you aren't crazy," she said.

"How can you be so sure?"

"Crazy people don't know they're crazy and you worry about it all the time."

Just in case, though, my parents thought I should move home. So at Thanksgiving, I did. At their suggestion, I went to see a psychologist (a first for my family) but after the second session, walked out more confused than healed. As the weeks passed, things did not improve. Even though I was surrounded by affection and support at home, no one seemed able to love me back to wellness. When I began to realize that there was no magic bullet, no instant cure to lift me out of my malaise, I got scared. If *they* couldn't help me, and *I* couldn't help me, who could? Believing that I had exhausted all of my resources and that my condition was permanent, I despaired until one day, the word "suicide" crossed my thoughts. This rattled my already fragile psyche even more. Fortunately, I had the presence of mind to step back and take a good, hard look at that word. Was it *loss* of life I wanted? Or was it *change* of life? I wanted change, of course. I just didn't know how to make that happen. I didn't know how to put hope back into my life.

To calm myself, I took to walking on the beach every morning and every night, even in the bitter cold. I also began praying when I woke up and just before bed. I didn't know much about praying, so I said the 23rd Psalm, then the Lord's Prayer, and even my childhood bedtime prayer. Sometimes I'd repeat the prayers two, even three times, for I was a sailor lost at sea, and these buoys were the only things left to cling to.

Shortly after the New Year, a childhood buddy stopped by and asked if I wanted to go fossil hunting at Calvert Cliffs.

"Fossil hunting in this weather? You must be insane," I said, ever hopeful for company.

"Come on. The fossils are amazing," he replied. "And it's so cold out no one will be there, so we'll probably find a lot of good stuff. Anyway," he said, looking at me still in my pajamas at noon, "you look like you could use some airing out."

I didn't have the energy to argue so I reluctantly pulled on some clothes, a parka and boots, and climbed into his car for the hour ride south.

Scientists and collectors favor Calvert Cliffs for the bounty of prehistoric fossils found there. This would be my first visit, but when we pulled into the empty parking lot I felt more nervous than excited. We hiked through nearly two miles of woods before reaching a clearing that opened onto a thin strip of uninteresting shoreline to our right and massive, eroding cliffs to our left. Before us spread a dull, gray panorama of cloudless sky and still water. The beach was deserted. The Bay, barren. There were no people, no birds, no fish, no boats. Nothing but me, my buddy and a great, ponderous silence.

I've never known such silence. It was infinite. All knowing. An ancient silence. One that had witnessed millions of years of transitions and transformations, births, deaths and renewals. This silence must be God, I thought. Here, all around me.

Standing in that silence by the vastness of the Bay, I felt so very small, and it occurred to me just how meager a fraction I was of the greater good. A mere speck of dust on the great screen of evolution. Next to this, the breadth of my life seemed so very short and my problems, worries and dashed hopes no more than "phfffts" on the fire.

As my companion headed toward the cliffs to look for fossils, I huddled by a pile of rocks in the sand. The rocks looked strange and otherworldly and I wondered what they had been in a past incarnation. A chunk from a Neolithic dwelling? A fragment of dinosaur bone? A piece of petrified tree? Fingering a fossil, I was reminded of a line from Roethke's poem, *The Far Field*: "Once I was something like this, mindless. Or perhaps with another mind, less peculiar."

These fossils represent such amazing transformations, I thought. Kind of like mine: from world traveler to sad sack. But maybe I can reincarnate, too, I thought. I can begin again. Erase and do over. Start fresh, like a newborn. Then another thought bubbled up unbidden— "what a peculiar word 'peculiar' is"—which made me giggle. Laughter. Always a good sign.

My buddy returned with a scallop shell the size of my hand. I'd never seen scallops in Chesapeake Bay before, and never any this size. I followed him back to the cliffs to search for more. An hour later, I was rewarded with two huge scallop shells. Then, hidden in the dark, wedged between two rocks, I discovered a large, whorled, charcoal-colored shell in near perfect condition. I tried to wriggle it free but it was stuck fast. So I pulled off my gloves and worked it gently with both hands, this way and that, until it finally came unstuck.

I felt an affinity for that snail shell and cradled it in my hands like a newborn chick all the way back to the car. I thought about all the upheavals and predators the shell had weathered in its lifetime: floods, ice, storms, droughts, megaladons, hunters, gatherers, (beachcombers). Yet it survived intact. Still, like me, it had been stuck in a dark place, unable to wrench itself free.

But you were not permanently stuck, little shell. If my hands hadn't wriggled you free just now, I believe that sometime in your future a large wave would have moved in, lifted you up and carried you on to a new place. Because that is the law of nature and the way of the beach, where life is not a condition of stasis but one of constant, if sometimes muted, change: the ebb and flow, high tide and low, loss and gain, death and rejuvenation. Each morning, the tides promise a new day, a new search, a fresh start. And when storms overwhelm the shore or shift the strandlines a few feet higher, remember: all bad weather eventually passes.

I learned that my shell was an *Ecphora*, the Maryland state fossil, from the Miocene period. Like the scallops, it was anywhere from 10 to 20 million years old.

That day at Calvert Cliffs marked the beginning of a *sea change*[3] in my thinking. "Out of these nothings, all beginnings come."[4] I began to see God all around me, in simple things like the light filtering through leaves, the horizon hovering protectively above water, in my dog's devotion and in everyday kindnesses. Somehow, as my faith in God grew, my feelings of hopelessness subsided. Yes, I had encountered my fair share of obstacles in the last 18 months but I would take old Andrew Barton's advice: "Fight on my men," says Sir Andrew Barton, "I am hurt but I am not slain; I'le lay me down and bleed a-while and then I'le rise and fight again!"[5]

So what if I couldn't afford to fast-track my education and return to a four-year college? There were other options. Community college, for instance. And maybe a retail or waitressing job to pay my tuition and commuting expenses. These choices didn't thrill me. But if I was going to change my life, I had to start somewhere. As the Chinese proverb suggests, "Be not afraid of going slowly. Be afraid only of standing still."

---

[3] A *sea change* denotes a noticeable transformation.
[4] Theodore Roethke again.
[5] Verse LXIV of *The Ballad of Sir Andrew Barton*, author unknown.

The next week I registered for two college courses. The week after that I was hired as a part-time waitress at a local jazz club. Taking on these commitments was scary but I knew if I didn't try them, I'd stay stuck. And I didn't much like being stuck.

Walking through the parking lot on that first day of class, I came upon a torn piece of paper that I picked up to throw away. On it was a picture of a hand pointing skyward and a spiritual quote. The image (now thumb-tacked to my bulletin board) reminded me that someone was watching over me, which provided me with enough confidence to get through that first day of class and many classes thereafter. By summer, I was back in the land of the living again with new friends, new interests and expanding opportunities.

My prehistoric shells from Calvert Cliffs are testimonies that the world has been spinning for a long, long time—*4.5 billion* years worth of time, in fact—which usually helps me maintain a healthy perspective during set-backs. I know now that, even when things look awful up close, it's the wider picture that counts. And, in that picture, I am blessed with important things: family, friends, good memories, my health. I know, too, that if I have faith, keep my eye on the prize and keep taking small steps, surely I will reach my goals.

The Consummate Beachcomber

Calvert Cliffs

Calvert Cliffs is one of the most productive and famous fossil areas in America. The cliffs extend 30 miles along the western shore of Chesapeake Bay, forming the longest stretch of exposed Miocene sediments on North America's east coast. Beaches here are littered with fossils from eroding cliffs and underwater outcrops.

Ten to 20 million years ago, during the middle Miocene epoch, a shallow ocean covered southern Maryland. Chesapeake Bay is the drowned Susquehanna River Valley. Calvert Cliffs are the eroded sides of that valley. Most of the fossil species found there represent three distinct formations—*Calvert, Choptank* and *St. Mary's*—all of which are from the middle Miocene epoch and are rich in shell, bone and teeth fossils. These fossils are from animals that inhabited the ancient sea or were washed into it, then sank to the bottom and were covered by sand. Erosion of a foot or two occurs every year because of landslides, storms and wave action, which undercut the base of the cliffs. When this happens, fossils fall from the cliffs into the water where they are tossed around and then cast back onto shore.

Current archaeological evidence suggests that the Patuxent River Indians of the Algonquin Nation were the first to collect and use fossils in their daily activities. Shark teeth modified into projectile points or scrapers, for instance, have been discovered during archaeological digs in the area. Spanish explorer Vincente Gonzales was probably the first European to spot the cliffs (1558) followed by Captain John Smith during his Bay explorations (1608). For the last 200 years, Calvert Cliffs has attracted geologists, naturalists and paleontologists from all over the world.

Although many of the beaches fronting Calvert Cliffs are private, the public can access the cliffs in a few places, including Calvert Cliffs State Park, though that involves a two-mile walk. Beachcombers are warned that climbing on or digging into the cliffs is illegal as people have been injured and even killed when large pieces of the cliff have broken off. Located nearby is Calvert Cliffs Nuclear Power Plant, which began generating electricity in 1975. The power plant has been rigorously monitored since its inception and, thus far, there has been no significant environmental damage or damage to marine life or zooplankton. So don't worry. If you wade in the water, you won't emerge glowing and neither will the fossils you find.

Miocene Fossils

A splendid diversity of fossils can be found at Calvert Cliffs including large barnacles, coral, whale bone and, the perpetual favorite, shark's teeth, especially the six-inch tooth from the *Carcharodon megalodon*,[1] an extinct relative of the great white shark. Although some modern gastropods also exist on the shores of Calvert Cliffs, beachcombers are mostly rewarded with fossil shells. These fossils can be readily identified because they are a chalky white and thicker than modern marine animals. Fossilized whalebone, dolphin bone, sharks teeth and scallop shells, on the other hand, are usually brown, reddish brown, gray or black.

Two sought-after fossils are the large, eye-catching scallop, *Chesapecten*, and the Maryland state fossil, the beautiful gastropod, *Ecphora gardnerae gardnerae*. Ecphora, a snail, is one of the more unusual fossils of the Miocene fauna in the mid-Atlantic region. It was also one of the first fossils from the New World to be illustrated in a European scientific work.[2] Characteristics of the ecphora include four strongly protruding ribs, a moderately wide *umbilicus*[3] and a russet-gray color that contrasts with the white color of other fossilized mollusks. Unlike most of today's snails, which are herbivores, ecphora were predatory univalves, boring holes in the shells of clams, scallops and other bivalves to feed on the mollusks inside. By the Pliocene period, two million years ago, all ecphora were extinct, probably as a result of global cooling.

---

[1]   Estimates suggest that the largest of these megalodons were 50 feet long and weighed about 50 tons (100,000 pounds)! That's a lot of shark.

[2]   A poor artistic rendition of ecphora first appeared in the 3rd edition of Martin Lister's Historiae Conchyliorum *History of Conchs* printed by William Huddesford in England in 1770.

[3]   An *umbilicus* is a hollow, cone-shaped feature that runs along the axis of a shell's coiling.

Chapter 14

Sea Trash to Beach Treasure

*Let rough times refine,
not define, you.*

*Sea gems from beaches on Delaware Bay,
Chesapeake Bay, Long Island, the Jersey Shore
and Kauai, Hawaii*

Lewes Beach, Delaware: *Sea Trash to Beach Treasure*

Let rough times refine, not define, you.

I don't know many beachcombers who can resist a piece of sand-washed glass when a wave tosses it up on shore. Such artifacts are just too lovely to ignore and I've amassed quite a collection of it over the years. Frosted, iridescent sea glass with smooth, rounded edges from ocean beaches. Moderately weathered beach glass, sometimes with legible characters embossed on them, plucked from the shores of rivers, lakes and bays. Opaque slivers of flat window glass in pale linen shades of lavender, beige, sea foam and ice blue. Precious sea-worn marbles, bottle stoppers and beads. And then there are sea gems: tiny, transparent orbs of frosted, colored glass that glisten like jewels.[1]

Sea gems represent hope to me, for theirs is the ultimate journey of survival and transformation. A journey that began eons ago with the gradual breakdown of quartz rocks into pebbles into miniscule grains of sand that, when heated to extraordinary temperatures, melt into a clear fluid—glass—that is molded, pressed or blown into bottles, bowls or beads. The water[2] glass you drink from is a product of this process. From rock to pebble to sand to liquid to a solid mass. Phew. How exhausting.

But the transformation process doesn't stop there; for what happens when the drinking glass breaks? If the shards are tossed into a bonfire, they melt and, when cooled, turn into sooty, sandy, dirty lumps of solid glass again. If they end up in a body of water—depending on the rigor of wave action, saline content, coarseness of sediment and duration in the water—the broken glass can evolve into a more refined, possibly more beautiful, reflection of its original form. The higher the salinity, the rougher the waves, the grittier the sediment, the longer the

---

[1] Sea gems are not to be confused with similar looking transparent orbs, which are quartz. I call these *button drops*. Others refer to them as *Cape Henelopen diamonds* or, in New Jersey, as *Cape May diamonds*. A chapter is devoted to button drops in *A Beachcomber's Odyssey, Volume II: Strands in the Sand* (also refer to Chapter 17).

[2] As an interesting aside, the water in that glass is the *same* water that has always been on earth though it has undergone many transformations in its several *billion* years of existence. Because the water molecule is too heavy to easily escape the earth's gravitational pull, almost every bit of water we drink, expell, flush, drain or dump comes back to help (or haunt) us again. To learn more about these and other fascinating facts related to the seashore, refer to one of my favorite books, *A Scientist at the Shore*, by James Trefil.

duration of time spent in the water, the smaller and more luminous the piece of glass becomes until, eventually, it transforms into a glittering gem from the sea.

I began collecting sea gems the summer I was 25 when Mother and I escaped the heat of central Maryland for the cool breezes of the Delaware shore. We started the day with an ocean swim at Cape Henelopen State Park, which offers a generous spread of long beaches, scrub pine and campgrounds. Then we drove to the sleepy, historic town of Lewes (pronounced Lewis) for lunch and a walk on a Delaware Bay beach. It was the first time in ages that I felt unreservedly happy. I think Mother felt the same, for both of us had weathered a very rough year.

Dad had taken ill and died the summer before, a heart-wrenching death; but at least Mother and I could navigate the turbulent waters of grief together. That fall we broke tradition and ate Thanksgiving dinner in a restaurant. The next week, a close family friend suffered a nervous breakdown and we visited her often, even on Christmas Day, at a psychiatric hospital near Baltimore. Then, on New Year's Eve, a college roommate called with news that my D.C. rental had caught fire and burned. So the first day of the snowy New Year was spent raking through the steaming rubble of what had once been my bedroom. The only unscathed item found was a cameo pin of an archangel carved on the surface of a piece of polished conch shell. A Guardian Angel that now rests with other treasures in my Trobriand Island box.

"Sea gems represent hope to me, for theirs is the ultimate journey of survival and transformation."

Six months later, with all that behind us, a happy day at the beach was cause for much celebration. We'd both gotten through a rough patch intact. Mother lost her spouse of 35 years but rose to the challenge of living by herself for the first time in her life. She was now traveling a bit and tending to her dog, her book club and her border gardens.

My rough patch lasted three years. After my return from the South Pacific, I'd fallen from the mountain's summit to (almost) rock bottom. Climbing back up had been a grind. But, in my case, Nietzsche's adage, "What does not destroy me, makes me stronger," proved true. For on that long trek back up the mountainside, I developed emotional muscle and learned to be more patient and discerning, and less judgmental.

But my transformation didn't stop there. My reticence over attending a community college and taking on a waitressing job to finance my education shifted 180 degrees. I discovered waitressing was fun and it suited me. I liked chatting people up and counting tips after hours. Working at the club also expanded my musical tastes to classic and Brazilian jazz through live performances by Charlie Byrd, Ethel Ennis and Earl "Fatha" Hines. Meanwhile, community college provided an affordable way to get back on the academic track. I met two of my favorite professors there and made a lifelong friend. How ironic that the very opportunities I'd originally overlooked proved imminently worthwhile. They even jump-started my life again. That fall I resumed my studies at a four-year college, on a partial scholarship, and waitressed to meet expenses.

So Mother and I both had blessings to count that day. A light-hearted, playful crowd was on Lewes Beach with balls and swim rafts, lacrosse sticks and kites. We chatted with everyone, talking more than beachcombing. But as we walked up the shoreline, little shimmers of light kept drawing our attention to the sand. I finally kneeled down to examine one. It was the smallest chip of beach glass I'd ever seen, no bigger than the head of a nail, sparkling in the palm of my hand like a diamond in a ring. Mother and I collected a score more during our walk and christened them "sea gems."

That night at home, I held the glass gems under a lamp, loving the way they glowed in the light. But their real beauty to me was what they represented. From rock to pebble to sand to glass to trash to tumbling fragment to treasure, they demonstrated how life could be an ever-evolving process of change and transformation. I could identify with their journey, a process not unlike what I'd undergone the last few years (though there are many, I'm sure, who would dispute my "gem-like" qualities). Yes, I'd hit a rough patch in my life but I finally emerged, battle worn but wiser, with my sharp edges smoothed down.

I've added many specimens to my sea gem collection since that first walk on Lewes Beach. In the morning light, their shimmer reminds me that what was once trash can evolve over time into diamonds, emeralds and aquamarines. Such gems may only be a poor man's jewels, but, to me, their shine is just as bright.

The Consummate Beachcomber

Lewes Beach on Delaware Bay

Lewes is located along Delaware Bay adjacent to Cape Henelopen, the point of land separating the Bay and the Atlantic Ocean. Evidence suggests that American Indians roamed through the area as far back as 12,000 BCE. By the time Europeans arrived in the region in the 1500s, groups from the Algonquin Nation (Siconese, Nanticoke, Lenni-Lenape) had settlements there.

European explorers from Spain and Portugal sailed along the Delaware coastline as early as 1529. English navigator Henry Hudson[1] is credited with the European discovery of the Delaware Bay and River in 1609, but the first European expedition to purposefully explore the Bay was captained in 1613 by Cornelius Hendricksen. He noted a heavily-forested region filled with deer and turkey, and traded with the Indians for skins of sable and mink. Nearly 20 years later, in 1631, Dutch immigrants arrived with food, cattle and whaling implements with the goal of turning a tract of land two miles wide and 32 miles long into farm plantations and whale fisheries. They established a permanent settlement named *Zwaanendael* (Valley of Swans) on *Hoorn Kill* (now Lewes Creek).[2] But within a year the settlement no longer existed. Allegedly, the settlers were killed and their buildings burned during a dispute with the Siconese Indians. But another, more recent, theory suggests that the men simply ran off to live with American Indian women. This assertion is based on an account that the physical appearance of some American Indians began to change around that time to towheads with blue eyes.

The town of Lewes was founded in 1659 and, over the next 200 years, played host to pirates (including Captain Kidd), smugglers, soldiers and colonial settlers. During the War of 1812, the town was bombarded by a convoy of British warships and it is reputed that one skilled frigate gunner managed to kill a chicken and wound an enemy pig!

Blessed with an excellent harbor, Lewes is still a seafaring town and home to a large fleet of charter fishing boats. It is also the southern terminus for the Cape May-Lewes Ferry. Fortunately, despite extensive real estate development along Delaware's Atlantic coast, this historic village has managed to retain much of its charming, small-town flavor and still offers visitors a wonderful place to holiday.

Sea Gems

By virtue of its fascinating past, Lewes Beach and neighboring Cape Henelopen provide beachcombers with a variety of things to look for in the sand. Atlantic clam shells, jingle shells and scallop shells are common. Ceramic shards and glass bottles are less common. Old coins and bottle stoppers are rare.

---

[1] Hudson was employed by the Dutch East India Trading Company. His many discoveries in the New World gave the Dutch the right to claim a significant portion of what is now the mid-Atlantic region.

[2] Today, the picturesque Zwaanendael Museum commemorates that first European settlement.

Fragments of glass can be plentiful, especially after storms or very high tides. Wave action repeatedly tumbles glass in a mixture of water and sand. The constant abrasion eventually dulls the glass's sharp edges and buffs, then frosts, its shiny surface until it is transluscent.

Factors such as wave action, grain size of the sand, salt content of the water, and age of the glass fragment can make a huge difference in the type and quality of glass found. With experience, one can learn to differentiate between various types of sea-worn glass, recently broken glass, melted bonfire glass and flat glass from broken windows. Coveted *sea glass* with smooth, rounded edges and a frosted surface is found most often on ocean beaches. *Sea gems* are transparent remnants of sea glass ground down to smooth, pearl-sized jewels. *Beach glass*, found along riverbanks or on shorelines fronting lakes, sounds or bays, is usually less frosted than sea glass because of weaker wave action and lower salt content. Beach glass fragments can be large and have legible writing or embossed designs on them. You may also find pieces that are frosted on one side and shiny on the other. This is probably because they were embedded in sediment, perhaps for hundreds of years, before finally being exposed.

'Combers may find that sea glass or beach glass is more plentiful in one location than another. Beaches situated near old dump sites or historically well-populated areas may yield substantial amounts of beach glass in a variety of colors. "Glass Beach" on Kaua'i, Hawai'i, remote west coast beaches, and shorelines along the Great Lakes (especially Lake Erie), New Jersey, Long Island Sound, Chesapeake Bay and Delaware Bay can be bountiful sources for all types of beach glass, especially if one searches on a coming low tide or after bad storms.

Sea glass, sea gems and beach glass come in all colors of the rainbow. Sea glass specialist, Richard LaMotte, has devised an excellent color ranking system in his reference book, *Pure Sea Glass*. The most common colors—kelly green, brown and white—are from beer and soda bottles. The popular shade of sea foam green comes from old Coca-Cola bottles. Cobalt blue can be from Milk of Magnesia bottles or Noxema face cream jars. Ice blue, amberina (a yellow-brown), olive green, teal, pink and lavender, though less common, can also be found on many beaches. Die-hard sea glass collectors especially covet rare colors such as orange, red, yellow and "black" glass (which is really a very, very dark green).

In the morning light, their shimmer reminds me
that what was once trash can evolve over time into diamonds,
emeralds and aquamarines. Such gems may only be a poor man's jewels,
but, to me, their shine is just as bright.

Chapter 15
The Windswept Shore

Tread lightly.

A turtle inkbottle discovered on a Virgina riverbank by the author's mother keeps company with two antique doorknobs from Orkney, Scotland.

Orkney, Scotland: *The Windswept Shore*

Tread lightly.

The world bristles and scrapes and hums at night with sounds of creatures moving in the dark. Ancient rhythms of animals—raccoon, deer, possum, fox—seeking food, water, shelter, a mate. I see their tracks in the sand in the early morning light when I walk the dog on the beach. Sometimes I also see slithery indentations from snakes shedding their skin or slipping through the sand seeking shelter before sunrise. Sometimes, too, I see death's ugly remnants—scattered bones and fur-covered hides—surrounded by a frenzy of paw prints. Animal patterns in the sand are not always pleasing.

Waves, wind and rain can also expose mysterious clues about human activity on the beach the night before or years ago. Chips of flaked stone. Fishing weights. Burned brick. Glass bottle stoppers. A lone high heel. Hmmm. It's been my experience that some beaches reveal more about our collective past than others. Like old souls, these beaches seem to groan under the weight of those who visited their shores centuries earlier: invaders, warriors, smugglers, pilgrims, priests, pirates and more.

The Orkney Islands, off the north coast of Scotland, have beaches like these. Their coastlines possess more life under their dunes and sand and rocky shores than almost any other place I've visited. These islands have a long history of human settlement, from Neolithic[1] peoples to Vikings to Scottish clan lords to war refugees escaping the terror of the Nazis. Remains of prehistoric occupation exist everywhere: standing stones and circles, earth houses, rock walls, even an underground village.

I was only remotely aware of such things the day I ferried there with Mother in 1978. It was late summer, the year after Dad died. I'd convinced her to accompany me on my research trip to Scotland. But first, I thought, we could explore the British Isles, her favorite part of the world. We spent a month driving from London to Wales and then back through the Cotswolds before venturing north through York to romantic Northumberland. Then we slowly moved

---

[1]   The Neolithic period ran from 8,000-3,200 BCE, the Bronze Age from 3,200-1,200 BCE and the Iron Age from 1,200-586 BCE.

on, roaming around Scotland's wildly magnificent west coast with its undulating lochs, castle ruins, rushing streams and fields of wild thistle. After making a spiritual journey to Iona by way of the Isle of Mull, we boarded a train at Inverness for the endless journey to Thurso on Scotland's north coast. The countryside grew bleaker the farther north we went, with miles of flat moorland and gorse. By the time we reached Thurso, we felt we'd come to the end of the earth. And there was still a ferry ride to take.

On the ferry I pulled out a detailed map of Orkney. The islands seemed like a world out of time. Ruled by Vikings for six centuries, even their place names—Hoy, Flotta, Eday—had an other-worldly sound, more Nordic than Scottish.[2] I learned the word Orkney itself was the shortened version of the Old Norse word *Orkneyjar*, or "Seal Islands." Cursory research yielded little current information about them. Aside from a naval base the British built and operated at Scapa Flow, Orcadians—like their northern sisters, the Shetlanders—had been left to themselves for a long, long time. Although I wasn't sure what to expect, I knew from past experience that, because they were islanders, they would be interesting. All people from sea-locked spheres are. Isolated from outside influences, they develop unique, idiosyncratic customs—some subtle, some pronounced—that set them delightfully apart from mainlanders.

Then, in the distance, I saw little islands. Breathtaking, windswept humps of treeless land. Big hills. A rugged coastline dotted with sandy beaches and stone walls and, beyond, a bucolic scene of verdant fields with grazing cows and stone *crofts* (farms). Mother and I disembarked at Stromness, one of two towns on Mainland, the largest island. Nearing the wharf, Stromness appeared almost storybook perfect: Lilliputian, with a quaint skyline of steep, pitched roofs. Solid. Sturdy. A bit stern, with narrow streets and hardy structures made of thick, stone blocks. As we made our way to a Bed and Breakfast, we passed rosy-cheeked men dressed in caps, Harris tweeds, oilskins and Wellington boots, all chatting in lyrical brogues.

We spent the first couple of days exploring Stromness and Kirkwall, the largest town on Mainland. In Kirkwall, we ate fish at an understated but elegant eatery, then strolled around the town. We were amused to see pedestrians stopping to admire a lone tree, set off by an ornate fence. It was as if the tree were a monument or an incredible work of art, which, when living in a treeless habitat, I suppose it actually was.

---

2   Orkney place names are mostly derived from Old Norse with only a handful possibly borrowed from Gaelic.

That Sunday Mother and I, along with another American, hopped on a bus to tour Skara Brae, a series of primitive Neolithic underground mound dwellings. The damp, misty morning made a compelling backdrop to the prehistoric settlement and I developed a new respect for the reserves of resilience and tenacity humans can call on when needed. That these people managed to carve out a viable life for themselves in such a remote, achingly lonely place— without the pleasure of goose down or hot water bottles or steel knives—and not just survive, but thrive, was almost incomprehensible. They'd obviously mastered the skills necessary to work within the confines of their limited environment. They'd certainly taken pains to build adequate nests to shelter themselves from the harsh elements. Obviously, too, they'd devised some sort of system—perhaps like the sophisticated Pacific island *tapu system*[3]—to prevent undue resource exploitation. Because the case for survival here is very clear: protect your habitat or die. It is a choice we humans have repeatedly faced throughout our history. These days, however, there aren't many new islands left to conquer or fresh fields left to develop. So our options come down to this: be pragmatic and protect our nest or be careless and perish.

After sobering Skara Brae, the three of us sat and waited an hour for a bus that never came. Finally we set out in the direction from whence we'd come hoping to connect with some form of transportation to return us to Stromness. Two hours and some miles later, we were still walk-ing. We'd moo-ed at a lot of cows and baaa-ed at some sheep. Sang some songs. Pitched some pennies. Kicked some stones. Still, no bus.

Thirsty and tired, we approached a lone croft hoping for a drink of water. An attractive, middle-aged woman answered the door.

Looking up, Mother gasped, "Greer Garson? The movie actress?"

"No," the woman replied.

"I'm sorry for asking," Mother said, "but you look just like her."

"Well, I guess I might," she replied, "since she's my first cousin. Americans are you? Here on holiday? Care for a cuppa tea?"

---

[3] *Tapu* (Tongan and Samoan) *kapu* (Hawaiian) or *taboo* (the bastardized European version of the word) all mean sacred and/or forbidden.

How quickly fortunes change. In a matter of minutes, we'd shifted from weary voyagers to guests of Greer Garson's cousin. We spent the next hour drinking milky hot tea, eating fresh-baked scones and leafing through scrapbooks of Greer when she was little. When we reluctantly took our leave, we did so with the new knowledge that buses stop running on Sunday afternoons and that our hostess was sorry but she didn't have a car. "Stromness is only a few miles down the road. You'll get there in no time. And here're some warm scones to hold you over. Cheerio!"

So off we wearily went, passing more cows, more sheep and a few young girls on horses. (I almost bribed one for a ride.) But still no cars, buses or adults. These are empty islands of land and sea with hardly a soul in sight. The emptiness takes a bit of getting used to and I was glad I had company, even if it was becoming increasingly cranky company.

A couple of miles later, we stopped at a ruin beside a long stone wall by a beach. While the others sat down to rest, I hopped over the wall to see what I could find in the sand. There wasn't much. A few uninteresting rocks. Some seaweed. Oh well. I was too tired to explore the beach anyway. All I really wanted to do was get some place where I could permanently put my feet up, but by the time I returned to the stone wall, my companions were snoring. Rather loudly, too. This wouldn't do. Nighttime was closing in and, though I could see Stromness in the distance, it still looked a good half hour's walk away.

Before waking them, I sat and ate a scone and toed some old rocks from the house ruin. I guess I kicked one rock fairly hard because it rolled off the pile exposing in the sand beneath a strange round object with a patina of silvery green. It was a tarnished old doorknob just like the ones on doors I'd seen throughout Stromness. It had probably come off a door from the croft that lay in ruins by the stone wall upon which Mother was now snoozing. My interest piqued, I got up and explored the area further. I didn't find much else though. A few rusted nails. A broken hinge. Then I came upon a second doorknob, this one prettier than the first. Heavier. More substantial.

Looking out at the empty beach and emptier sea, it was hard to believe that anyone other than us had ever walked these silent shores. But people had not only walked them, they'd fished from them and lived beside them, and probably raised children who played on them, and owned cows and horses who grazed beside them. These former crofters—like their prehistoric ancestors—were not necessarily considerate caretakers of their world. After all, they left behind old doorknobs for me to find. But they didn't leave much else or, if they did leave trash, it slowly disappeared because it was biodegradable. They didn't have the kind of environmental pressures or ecological dilemmas we face today. No plastics. No traffic jams. No aerosol sprays or packing peanuts. Their footprints were very small indeed. A stone wall. A crumbling ruin. An unblemished beach. A clean sea. And two very tarnished old doorknobs.

By the time we reached Stromness, it was nearing dark and our legs were wobbly. Mother and I took long baths, ate supper, and then watched the telly with the elderly owners of the tidy Bed and Breakfast. When I showed them the doorknobs I found, they had a good laugh.

"You crazy American! What can you be thinkin', collectin' such worthless trash?"

"Well now," I said, "there's trash and then there's *trash*."

"Nonsense! It's all trash to me," the wife said.

And I could tell she didn't get it. Because to me, the doorknobs were not trash but "memory tokens" that could transport me back someday to a time in my life when I was a fit, adventurous 26-year-old experiencing a windswept world with someone I loved. A pristine island world inhabited by conscientious caretakers.

These days my Orkney doorknobs symbolize some very good memories. They also fortify my resolve to live with an "island mentality," because pretending that my space in the world is limited encourages me to keep my footprint small. To do this, I rely on those time-tested Yankee values of resourcefulness, recycling and never buying more than I need (unless, of course, it's on sale...).

The beach is as good a place as any to start being a steward of the world. Here, earth care revolves around simple beachcombing etiquette: don't take more than you need; share or trade what you find; and, sometimes, tote an extra bag along to collect trash. In my beachcombing workshops, I encourage participants to protect the shore's gentle ecology. Don't trample dune grass, or kill mollusks for their shells, or gouge reefs for coral or cliffs for fossils. Except for sandy footprints, don't leave a trace of yourself behind. No drink cans, cigarette butts or plastic. If you must dig in the sand, fill the hole back up when you're through. But also remember, if you have to dig for something, it really isn't beachcombing.

My doorknobs now rest on a mantle alongside an old turtle-shaped inkbottle Mother found on a Virginia riverbank. Whenever I notice them, I feel the beat of the world's ancient rhythms and hear the bristles and scrapes and hums of creatures moving in the night. With our help, may such vibrations continue for centuries to come.

The Consummate Beachcomber

Orkney Islands

The Orkney Islands are located in the North Atlantic, 20 miles off the north coast of Scotland and 50 miles south of Greenland. The islands cover 376 square miles with approximately 570 miles of coast-line. Orkney comprises 70 islands though only 17 are inhabited. With a population close to 20,000, the majority of Orcadians live on the largest island, Mainland, a name derived from the Old Norse word *Meginland*.

Orkney was formed from the glacial erosion of underlying limestone, sandstone and igneous rock that evolved into low, undulating hills covered by glacial deposits. Today peat and extensive grazing lands cover the islands and, though the climate is relatively mild, frequent winds and strong gales account for the scarcity of trees.

An archaeologist's dream, the island chain offers extensive evidence of human occupation beginning more than 5,000 years ago, from the Neolithic Period through the Bronze Age to the Pictish people during the Iron Age. One site, Minehowe, is a mysterious subterranean chamber dug deep into an earthen mound. Another impressive site, the underground village of Skara Brae,[1] is one of Europe's most complete relics of the late Neolithic Period. And there are so many neolithic tombs on the island of Rousay that it is known as "the Egypt of the North."

The 7th century marked the arrival of Celtic missionaries, followed by Norse raiders in the 8th and 9th centuries looking for farmland. The Norsemen colonized and ruled the islands for the next 600 years. Then, in 1472, Orkney, along with the Shetland Islands, passed into Scottish rule and today the islands are governed by Scotland, belong to Great Britain and are part of the European Union.

Over the last century, depopulation has periodically occurred as men left Orkney searching for a means to support their families. The father of beloved American essayist Washington Irving was an Orcadian who left the islands under the employ of the Hudson Bay Company. At one point in that company's history, seven out of 10 employees were Orcadians.

[1] Skara Brae and several other sites in Orkney including the Stones of Stenness, Ring of Brogar and Maes Howe have collectively been designated a UNESCO World Heritage Site.

"Breathtaking, windswept humps of treeless land. Big hills.
A rugged coastline dotted with sandy beaches and stone walls and,
beyond, a bucolic scene of verdant fields with grazing cows and stone crofts."

S. Deacon Ritterbush photo archives

During WWI and WWII Orkney served as a British naval base. In the 1970s the development of the North Sea oil industry created a limited amount of employment opportunities but farming provided the leading source of income. Although the island boasts its fair share of peat and moorland, more and more land has been claimed for agriculture and Orcadian farmers supply the Scottish mainland with a fair share of beef, eggs, milk and potatoes.

Doorknobs

The range of items I've discovered beachcombing is always a source of amazement to me. And the research journeys I've traveled to learn more about specific artifacts can be very entertaining. No matter how rare or esoteric the treasure, there are experts or associations somewhere in the world who can shed light on my discoveries. So it is with old metal doorknobs.

Clearly, the purpose of doors is to close off the interior of dwellings from the outside environment. In ancient cultures, doors were made of hides, woven reeds, wood or textiles. One wonders what the Picts and Vikings used in the treeless Orkneys to close off the entry ways of their underground shelters. Slabs of rock? Pieces of driftwood lashed together? Maybe even frozen turf?

Since the 1700s, doorknobs in the shape of a lever, a ball or an egg-shaped sphere have opened most entry ways in Europe. The doorknobs came in a variety of materials including wood, glass, ceramic or metal. In the Victorian era porcelain knobs were popular. But the best grade of doorknobs were made of bronze[2] or brass.[3]

Begninning in the 1800s, metal doorknobs were *cast*—poured into a mold—or *forged*, a more economical and efficient process where heated metal is forced into shaped dies. Forging produces especially high quality products that are tough, reliable and of superior strength. The use of brass for doorknobs became widespread during the late Victorian era. Many of these doorknobs had beautifully detailed ornamental designs. Today, more than 1,000 antique doorknob designs—sorted into 15 types based on shape, design and material—have been documented.

The dented, lightweight doorknob I found on Orkney is brass. The heavier, smoother doorknob is bronze.

[2] Bronze, which is 80% copper and 20% tin, is a very hard metal with long-lasting capabilities.
[3] Brass, a softer metal that is 60% copper and 40% zinc, is easy to tool and has an excellent ability to resist rust .

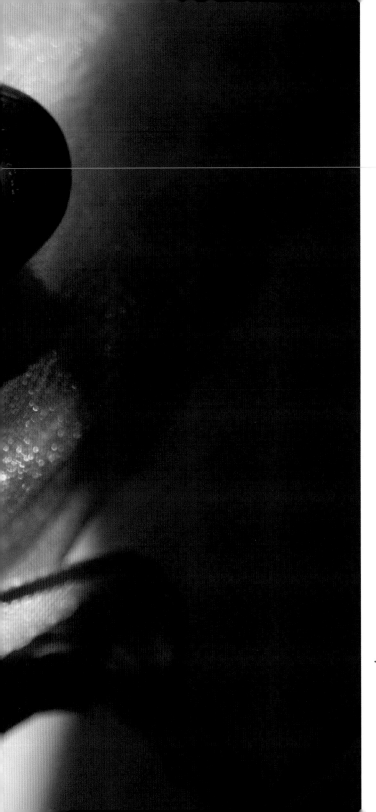

Chapter 16
Storm Surges

*Distraction is a
cure for almost any ill.*

*An ancient serpentine and red sandstone rock
from Scotland's Shetland Islands with a geologic
etching on it reminiscent of Nantucket Island*

Shetland Islands, Scotland: *Storm Surges*

Distraction is a cure for almost any ill.

I have just landed on Unst, a remote island in the great North Sea. It's like being on the moon, but in a good way. Wide-open and treeless, with a sky so big its cool, pale light brightens every barren hillock, maroon peat bog and field of purple heather. There are lots of teeny Shetland ponies and dogs (called *shelties*) on Unst, flocks of sea birds, and plain sturdy crofts of gray or whitewash stone with walls nearly two feet thick.

Unst is the northernmost island in the remote Shetland Islands. Located 50 miles north of the Orkneys and 400 miles south of the Arctic, it took three bus trips and two ferry rides to get here from Lerwick, a city on Mainland, the largest of the Shetland Islands.

A few weeks back, I'd put Mother on a ferry to Thurso for her return to America. I left the following week to research the impact of the North Sea oil industry on the traditional Shetland way of life. After a very rough ferry trip up from Orkney, reaching Shetland was a godsend, a dream of stunning black islands in a swirling silver sea. The map showed even stranger names than Orkney: Yell, Uyeasound, Papa Stour, Muckle Flugga.[1]

Cosmopolitan Lerwick felt like a gold rush town in the Wild West. It was overrun with an international contingent of oilmen, engineers, speculators and investors looking to divvy up a piece of the black-gold cake. The city's cold stone buildings, busyness and traffic noise also diluted the thrill I'd felt when I first saw the islands. It was difficult to get a sense of the Shetlanders' insular, more traditional way of life, though their lilting accents and dry humor entertained me every night as I ate dinner in the pubs. Whenever I mentioned my research undertaking, locals always urged me to visit Unst, not only for its beauty and isolation, but also because they regarded it as the most traditional of the Shetland Islands.

So I packed my bags and here I am. Unst is colder than Mainland. It feels less like late August and more like October. I book myself into Gardiesfauld youth hostel in Uyeasound. The hostel is on a small hill overlooking a bay. I deposit my duffel in a corner room upstairs, pull on

---

[1]   The most northerly point in the United Kingdom, Muckle Flugga, a mile off the coast of Unst, is little more than a lighthouse and a pile of rocks.

a second sweater, retrieve some cheese, an apple and a tea bag from my knapsack, and head to the kitchen to boil water. There I meet a motley but congenial crew of hostelers: an Irish girl from County Sligo, an English boy from Nottingham, an East Indian woman from London, and an American fiddler from West Virginia visiting Unst with the hope of playing with some of the "best fiddlers in the world." There are other people staying in the hostel, too: graduate students studying Unst's famous rare birds, and a couple of others off drinking at a pub in Baltasound, the island's largest town (which isn't saying much).

The hostellers seem well acquainted and comfortable with each other. As the newcomer, I am a bit shy, a shyness that soon turns to unease when the hostel manager appears at the front door to warn us that a "big blow" is on its way with winds up to 140 miles an hour.

"No cause for alarm," he assures us. "Big blows come frequently and these dwellings are sturdy enough to withstand 'em. If the electric goes out, there're matches on the mantle and enough peat by the hearth for a tidy fire that should see you through the night. But once the blow starts," he cautions as he turns to leave, "it's best you stay inside and keep clear of fallin' objects should the house start tremblin' from all the air." With a wave, he departs.

The news excites the boys, who consider it the next great adventure. The girls seem more apprehensive. I look out the window at a sea already choppy and turning as dark as the sky above it. I'm thinking, they call 140-mile-per-hour winds here a "Big Blow?!" Why, in my neck of the woods, that's a *Category Four hurricane!*[2] Damn, I thought, it's going to be a long night and here I am, stuck on a midget island in the middle of nowhere with a bunch of strangers, no food and a "Big Blow" coming. The slow crawl of anxiety—the one that gives me that creepy feeling of being simultaneously trapped and restless and in great need of air—starts to climb up my spine. Intellectually, I know that fear is a choice of mind over matter. But, for people like me with over-active imaginations, the mind is what usually causes the problem and turning it off can sometimes be tricky. Reminding myself that fear happens more in the anticipation of something then in its actuality doesn't help much.

2   Category Four hurricanes have wind speeds of 131 to 155 mph and storm surges up to 18 feet. Homes may suffer extensive damage, trees may be uprooted and extensive flooding can occur. Even Category Three hurricanes, with winds up to 130 mph, can demolish large trees and even trailer homes.

To quell the rising panic, I have two choices: run upstairs and climb under the covers or head outside to explore the beach before the storm hits full force. I choose option two and race upstairs, pull on a windbreaker, stuff a flashlight in my pocket, grab my wallet and passport (because, well, you never know…) and run outside. Maybe the waves will wash in a Bronze Age relic (such a dreamer) or at least an interesting rock, for which Unst is famous.

The wind is picking up and the temperature has dropped. A few children run playfully about with open umbrellas, hoping the stiff breeze will lift them high enough to fly, Mary-Poppins-style. Watching them amuses me and, by the time I reach the water's edge, I've forgotten to feel scared.

I search the bay for otters and seals, but all I see are white-capped waves crashing against the wharf. So I turn to the shoreline with rocks colored the same dark maroon as the island's peat

> *"In my hand I hold a rock that transports me*
> *thousands of miles across the Atlantic to a piece of my world.*
> *And I am comforted."*

bogs. Many stones are medium size, well worn and smooth to the touch, with a sheen probably acquired from millions of years of churning in the sea and sand.

I come upon one stone with a mustard-yellow mark on it. A familiar mark. Miraculous, really, because it resembles a map of Nantucket. In my hand I hold a rock that transports me thousands of miles across the Atlantic to a piece of my world. And I am comforted.

By now, the light is fading. The wind gusts are so powerful now they nearly knock me down. Time to head back to the hostel. But on my return, I meet up with the other hostelers, including the two birdwatchers (but not the pub crawlers) on their way to the wharf to experience the big blow first hand. "Come on," they say, and someone grabs my hand. On the wharf we hunch low against the wind, link arms and walk partway out, forming a human chain that stretches from side to side. We scream at the top of our lungs as sea spray washes over us and micro bursts of air buffet us back and forth like rag dolls. One person is nearly blown off the wharf into the cold, restless water below. How crazy is this, I think? Pretty crazy the hostel manager says as he rushes down and shoos us back inside, "You bloody fools! It's a wild, willy wind out here.[3] Get along now."

Two hours later, the electricity out, we huddle around the firelight sharing food and swapping stories above the wind's roar. Suddenly, there's a loud bang and we turn to see three ghoulish figures appear in the doorway, their hair standing on end and their faces a sickly green. It's the pub crawlers! All very drunk indeed. So drunk they were stupid enough to walk miles through a big blow and numb enough to survive it. One holds a bottle of whiskey, another some beer and the third, a fiddle. "I told you we'd find you a fiddler!" they say to the American. And soon, a fiddling frenzy begins with the rest of us dancing and clapping and laughing all through the night as the wild, willy winds blow on and on and on…

3   Other wonderful local expressions include *da peerie fokk* (fairies) and *da simmer dim* (mid-summer twilight).

The Consummate Beachcomber

Shetland Islands
The Shetland Islands are a group of 100 nearly treeless, low-lying islands located in the North Atlantic, midway between Scotland and Norway. Fewer than 30 of these starkly beautiful islands are inhabited. Shetland has some of the most varied and complex geography and geology found anywhere in the United Kingdom. Major landforms survive from before the Ice Age. Millions of years of sculpting from seas, rivers, glaciers and erosion have created a fascinating and varied landscape. This includes expansive moorland; deep, indented coastlines; cliffs on the outer coasts and, along the inner coasts, sandy beaches, bogs, bays and *voes* (sea lochs) surrounded by steep hills. Winds are strong and nearly continuous and severe storms are frequent. But the warming Gulf Stream system creates a humid climate that is surprisingly mild for such high latitude.

Like Orkney, these islands are an archaeologist's paradise. Prehistoric settlements indicated by stone circles and *brochs* (circular unmortared towers) suggest that the islands were probably first settled by Picts. Jarlshof[1] on Mainland, an area continuously occupied from the Bronze Age (3,200 BCE to 1,200 BCE), is a time capsule of Shetland life. During the 7th or 8th century, missionaries from Ireland or Western Scotland arrived to convert the heathen Picts to Christianity. But, as in Orkney, land-hungry Vikings put an end to these activities sometime in the 8th or 9th century. These Norse invaders ruled

1   Jarlshof, a name coined by Sir Walter Scott in his 1822 novel, *The Pirate*, is one of Europe's most comprehensive archaeological sites, with examples of human settlement ranging from the Stone, Bronze and Iron Ages through the Pictish, Norse and Medieval periods.

the region for the next 600 years until King Christian I of Denmark, Norway and Sweden sold them to James III of Scotland. For centuries the geographically-isolated islands offered a safe haven for pirates and smugglers, both of whom probably turned a profitable penny trading contraband.

Although the Shetlands were incorporated into the Kingdom of Scotland in 1472 and are now a part of the United Kingdom, they have always stood apart from mainstream Scottish history and traditions. This is due both to their remote location and to their long association with Scandinavia. Until the 18th century the principal language of the islands was *Norn*, derived from Old Norse. Throughout much of the 20th century Shetland islanders lived a relatively quiet life of fishing, farming and animal husbandry. They raised world-renowned native breeds of sheepdogs; hardy, tiny-proportioned ponies; and sheep whose coats produced a soft, fine wool that was knitted into *Fair Isle* sweaters with colorful yoke designs reputedly copied from clothing worn by Spanish sailors who shipwrecked there in 1588.

Although Shetland sheltered many refugees from Norway during WWI and WWII, it was not until the discovery of North Sea oil and the construction of an oil terminal in the 1970s that the modern world began to encroach on the islanders' insular way of life. Today many Shetlanders earn their income from employment related to the oil industry as well as from fishing and tourism.

Unst, the most northerly populated island in the British Isles, has more than its share of archeological relics. But it is Unst's unique, scenic and varied topography and wildlife habitats that attract naturalists, bird-watchers and geologists from around the world. Home to two nature reserves, the island boasts 60 square miles of rugged cliffs, rocky shores, dunes, sandy beaches, peat bogs, moors, freshwater lochs and even a sub-arctic stony desert. This varied habitat plays host to sea bird colonies, otters, seals and, occasionally, summering whales and dolphins. Unst is also home to a *blanket bog*, an internationally rare habitat that provides excellent breeding grounds for a number of rare bird species including the great skua and the red-throated diver. A mile off Unst's north coast is the small island of Muckle Flugga, whose lighthouse was built by Thomas and David Stevenson, father and uncle of author Robert Louis Stevenson. Stevenson himself visited the island in 1869 when he was 19 and some suspect that Unst was the inspiration for his book, *Treasure Island*, as its shape closely resembles the treasure map in the book.

Rocks

Composed of ancient metamorphic, sedimentary and volcanic rocks, Unst is a geologist's paradise. Although the beachcomber on Unst may be lucky enough to find pieces of pottery, fishing floats or a pirate's doubloon, more likely they will find rocks, rocks and more rocks. Serpentine and gabbroic rocks, which were once part of an ancient ocean sea floor, are common. In fact, the island boasts the largest outcrop of serpentine rock in Europe. Chromite, a rock that can be crushed and used for making explosives, yellow paint and metal plating, is also common. The collector can find chunks of granite, greenstone and red sandstone. Soapstone, which the Vikings carved into bowls and utensils more than a thousand years ago, is also abundant.

"...reaching Shetland was a godsend; a dream of stunning black islands in a swirling silver sea..."

S. Deacon Ritterbush photo archives

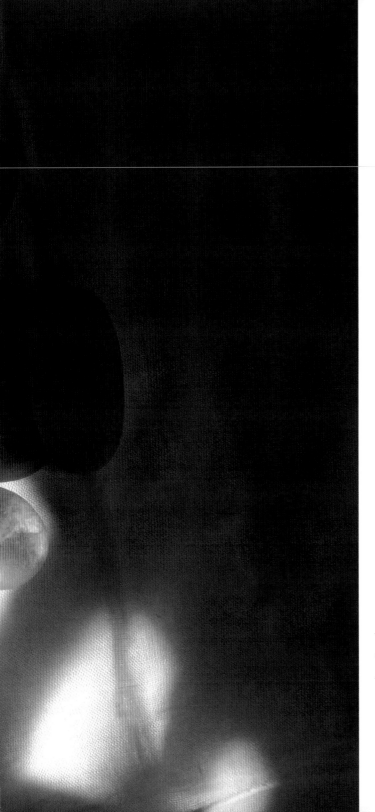

Chapter 17
The Edge of Thin Water

Death is always new.

A pink, heart-shaped oyster shell and rose quartz from beaches near Annapolis, Maryland

Annapolis, Maryland: *The Edge of Thin Water*

Death is always new.

Of all the beautiful objects I've discovered in my years of beachcombing, my favorites are still the smoothed disks of sunrise quartz I find on beaches near my home. I covet them, not because they are rare or of special design, but because their warm, soothing shades of shell pink, rose and salmon remind me of good things: new beginnings, late spring flowers and a mother's love. Ironically, the summer I began collecting them was the saddest of my life. It was the summer Mother died.

The year after our trip to the United Kingdom, I moved to Hawai'i to attend graduate school. It never occurred to me that the U.K. trip would be the last Mother and I would take together. The following year, on Valentine's Day, she sent me a care package containing my favorite cheap chocolate, a pink, heart-shaped oyster shell she'd found on our beach and a festive card that read, "Take My Heart." Pleased, I propped the shell and card on a table, ate some candy and left for a game of volleyball. I returned two hours later to learn that Mother had just suffered a massive heart attack.

Like a ship in a rough sea, my world heaved sideways, never to fully right itself again.

I withdrew from school and flew home to care for her. That spring, as Mother grew stronger, she shifted to the outside chaise where I'd cover her in blankets and, together, we'd sit in the sunshine watching kids with their dogs play on the beach. Sometimes I invited her friends over for afternoon tea and listened as they talked gardens or books or giggled over local goings-on. And there were many nights when, curled up beside her on her bed, we laughed as she recounted my crazy childhood escapades, and I asked her questions I feared I might never have the chance to ask later: how she met Dad; how to tell when I've met "the right one"; what she regretted not doing; who her heroes were and why?

But try as hard as she could, it seemed her big, old heart had had just about enough of life. It's not easy watching someone you love so much struggle so hard to stay alive.

One day, on my way up the hill from beachcombing, a neighbor called out to say that Mother had just been rushed to the hospital. Over the next three weeks, I watched her condition worsen until she slowly drifted off into a coma and finally slipped away into what I could only believe were God's loving arms. A vague kind of numbness protected me as I left the hospital that day and drove home through a terrible thunderstorm. It was as if the skies were weeping, too.

That first night without Mother felt surreal. I lay on her bed, my nose pressed into the pillows, smelling her familiar scent of Bond Street perfume mingled with lavender sachet. The night-gown she'd worn the morning before entering the hospital was still draped over the rocking chair and her beloved dog Copey slept soundly on the bedside floor, just as he had every night since Dad died. For a few seconds, I allowed myself to believe that nothing had changed; that the person and the life I'd always known and loved were not gone. But in my heart, I knew they were gone. A forever kind of gone.

"Dying pulls you, like the edge of thin water, ever so slowly out to sea, farther and farther away from the people you love, until they become only specks on a distant shore."

The busyness of the next few weeks left me numb. There was the funeral to plan. The dog to feed. Phone calls to answer. Bills to pay. Sixty years worth of possessions to sort and pack. Still, grief managed to find me at the most awkward times: standing in line at the grocery store, watching TV with friends, or even idling in the car at a red light. I chastised myself for not handling things better; after all, death was nothing new. I'd been through it before and was well acquainted with the kaleidoscope patterns of grief: the anger and remorse, the guilt and laughter, all swirling around crazily inside of me. But I soon came to understand that, no matter how many times we experience it, no matter how seasoned or prepared we think we are, "The death of a loved one," as the African proverb says, "is always new." And it's up to us to find a way to get through it. Somehow.

When my grief became too much, I'd walk to the beach and lie at the "edge of thin water" as Mother once called it; that place where the waves gently but persistently pull you into deeper water if you let them. "That's how dying feels," she had said months earlier. "Dying pulls you, like the edge of thin water, ever so slowly out to sea, farther and farther away from the people you love, until they become only specks on a distant shore."

Curled in the Bay's thin, warm film of wetness did not make my yearning for Mother go away but, somehow, it always seemed to bring me closer to her.

After one particularly sleepless night, I trudged to the beach before dawn and lay again by the water's edge. Slowly, as the sun rose, the world enveloped me in its soft pink blanket of sunrise. Wrapped in that cloak of morning, I felt hopeful for the first time in weeks and finally got up to walk the beach. As I walked, I began to notice all the life going on around me: morning joggers and dog walkers, noisy osprey teaching their young to fish, watermen hauling up traps teeming with blue crab.

When I climbed over one jetty to the next beach, my foot landed beside a large flat stone of pink quartz, the same shade as the dawn sky or mother's cheeks after a hearty laugh. I picked it up and, as I walked, I rubbed its comforting coolness between my fingers. My first sunrise quartz.

That same day, a letter came from a friend, recently widowed. She wrote, "Pain is like deep water. You cannot fight it. You cannot yield yourself to it. You can only work your way calmly and steadily through it, and so at last come to peace."[1] Like a balm, I rubbed her words over and over again into my heart, the same way I rubbed the sunrise quartz between my fingers.

As if by premonition, the month before mother died, she said not to worry; that there would always be substitutes. Athough I've run into some pretty good pinch hitters over the years, I've never found a substitute for her. But with time, the ache from deep loss, like a slow swell rolling out to sea, has subsided.

Beyond the passing of time, what moved me forward most was remembering that I was her gift to the world. A poem I found in her journal also helped:

[1]   Written by my dear friend, the late Roberta Whitehead Mikules, author of children's books published in the mid-20th century

If I should die and leave you,
Be not like others, quick undone
Who keep long vigil by the
Silent dust and weep.
For my sake turn to life and smile
Nerving thy heart and trembling hand
To comfort weaker souls than thee.
Complete these unfinished tasks of mine
And I perchance may therein comfort thee.[2]

As a way to honor her love for me, I began serving others more. Doing this eased my loneliness and loss like nothing else had,[3] though moments still come, even now, when I miss her to tears. The heart mends, after all, but it never really forgets.

I have many beautiful sunrise quartz now. To make them glisten, I keep them in a glass bowl filled with water. All, that is, except for that first quartz I found that summer mother died. It travels with me wherever I go and has been rubbed so much, it has a glow all its own.

---

[2] *If I Should Die* by English poet Thomas Gray (1716-1771)
[3] Perhaps because "The best excercise for the human heart is to bend down and lift someone else up," an apt sentiment expressed by T.V. commentator, Tim Russert (1950-2008), who died while this book was in production.

The Consummate Beachcomber

Historic Annapolis
Located on the Severn River and overlooking Chesapeake Bay, Annapolis—along with Newport, Rhode Island and Charleston, South Carolina—is a crown jewel of America's historic seafaring towns. The city is many things to many people. Self-proclaimed sailing capital of America, it is a port of call for sailors manning boats of all shapes, styles and sizes. Former home to four signers of the Declaration of Independence, Annapolis is also where African Kunte Kinte, immortalized in Alex Haley's book, *Roots*, was sold into servitude. A leader in historic preservation, the city serves as a showplace of some of the nation's finest examples of Georgian architecture. (1739-1775) It is also a college town to two of America's finest undergraduate institutions: St. John's College and the U.S. Naval Academy.

Annapolis was founded in the 1640s by a group of militant puritans migrating north from Virginia. Originally called Providence, the small settlement became known a few years later as Anne Arundel Town, named after the wife of the second Lord Baltimore. In 1695 Francis Nicholson, the 2nd Royal Governor, moved the seat of government there from St. Mary's City, renaming the town "Annapolis" in honor of Princess Anne. Fifteen years later, in 1708, as Queen Anne, she formally incorporated Annapolis and granted it a municipal charter.

The design for the state capital, which was inspired by European capitals and the gardens of Versailles, consisted of a Baroque plan of streets radiating from two circles. The domed State Capital,[1] oldest in the nation in continuous legislative use, reigns on a circle on the highest hill in the city. The Episcopal Church—formerly the Anglican Church—sits at the top of Main Street on the adjacent circle. When first built, both building sites had advantageous views of the port at the bottom of the hill.

Prior to the American Revolution, Annapolis was an important and prosperous seaport. During this era of wealth and privilege, planters of the *golden leaf* (tobacco) made so much money they could afford to build magnificent townhouses in competition with resident trade barons and aristocrats. This competition resulted in the construction of some of America's most resplendent homes from the late Georgian period.[2]

In 1774, just before the outset of the American Revolution, militant city patriots burned the brig *Peggy Stewart* in protest against British-imposed import taxes. During the Revolutionary War (1775-1783), Annapolis served as the administrative center of Maryland's war effort and became the nation's Capitol for a brief period after the war. During this time, George Washington resigned his commission as Commander-in-Chief before the Continental Congress (1783) and, in 1784, the Treaty of Paris—ending the Revolution and establishing America as a new nation—was ratified.

Eighty years later, during the Civil War, the city served as an administrative center for the Union Army's war effort. After that war, the city entered into a quiet century of genteel living replete with oyster shucking at the market place, Midshipmen walking in formation en route to church, and produce stalls and snowball stands making a brisk income during hot, humid summers.

In 1965 downtown Annapolis was designated a National Historic Landmark District and today, tourists and scholars alike come from all over the world to visit. Still a legendary port of call, Annapolis has a thriving maritime industry supported by several yacht clubs, sailing associations, and yearly motor and sailboat shows that attract thousands. At any time of the year, people explore the city's back streets,

---

[1] The first statehouse, built after the town was platted in 1696, burned in 1704. A second statehouse was completed in 1706. That statehouse was torn down and replaced in 1772 with the one standing today.

[2] Examples of these homes include the Hammond-Harwood house, Paca house, Chase-Lloyd house and Acton Place.

eat crab cakes, browse through antique shops on Maryland Avenue, and feed ducks at city dock near a statue of author Alex Haley reading of Kunte Kinte's adventures to an enthralled group of bronzed children.

Quartz

Just like the chocolate flamed Venus clamshell in Tonga, there are so many quartz stones on Chesapeake Bay beaches that people take them for granted and most passersby ignore them. But to me, the overlooked quartz stone is a special treasure on Chesapeake beaches because of its calming colors and cool, silky-smooth surface. One of the most varied minerals on earth, quartz is extremely common. It can be found in all geologic environments and is an important constituent of many rocks. On a scale of one to 10, quartz ranks 7th in hardness. (Diamonds rank 10th.) Quartz comes in many forms and in a wide range of colors including white, purple, pink, gray, yellow and brown. Some specimens can be multicolored, banded, transparent or opaque.

There are two major classifications of quartz. *Cryptocrystalline* has microscopic crystals that are translucent or opaque. Agate, bloodstone, jasper, carnelian, onyx and tiger's eye are examples of this type of quartz. The cellular contents of petrified wood and dinosaur bone are actually composed of cryptocrystalline quartz. The other type of quartz, *Crystalline* quartz, is always transparent and occurs in distinct crystals distinguished by color. Examples of crystalline quartz include rock crystal and semi-precious gems such as amethyst, citrene, smokey quartz and rose quartz.

Chesapeake Bay beaches are made up of billions of miniscule quartz grains. The quartz stones found on Bay beaches come in a variety of shapes and sizes including tubular, round, oval or flat shapes. Common colors include yellow, amber, brown or milky white. Occasionally you may find quartz in shades of pink, deep rose, orange, gray. or translucent.

Along with rose quartz, I also collect *old man's toenails* (smooth, thin ovals of quartz) and *button drops*[3] (small, transparent quartz pebbles) while beachcombers from Massachusetts' Cape Cod region collect milky white quartz pebbles, which they call *magic pebbles*[4] because they glow when tapped together.

[3]   *Button drops, Cape May diamonds* and *Cape Henelopen diamonds* are favorite treasures of Maryland, New Jersey, and Delaware beachcombers. People often incorrectly identify them as sea glass but they are really pure, translucent quartz crystals. Sizes range from tiny, sea-gem size to larger than a marble. These button drop quartz are usually colorless, like diamonds, but I have also found some that are smoky gray and pink. When polished, they gleam like crystal and some are even faceted into pieces of jewelry.
[4]   Refer to Robert N. Oldale's article, "Cape Cod's 'Magic' Quartz Pebbles," in the 1997 *The Cape Naturalist*.

Chapter 18
Sea Dreams

Lie back and the sea will hold you.

A weatherworn glass fishing float found on a beach near Waikiki, O'ahu

Waikiki, Hawai'i: *Sea Dreams*

Lie back and the sea will hold you.

There's a beach I visited often when I was in graduate school in Hawai'i. Nicknamed *Sans Souci* (French for "carefree"), it is located in Waikiki at the edge of Kapiolani Park. It is a small beach, wedged between a hotel and the crumbling Natatorium where our first cinematic Tarzan, Johnny Weissmuller, performed diving exhibitions in the 1940s. Tourists rarely stray that far from central Waikiki, so locals consider Sans Souci *their* beach and use it daily to swim, have barbecues, or just sit on the seawall watching all the beautiful people strut their stuff. (Hence the beach's nickname, "Dig Me Beach.")

People don't do much beachcombing on Sans Souci because there's not a lot to find. Instead, they come to sun themselves, smell the salt air, lie back and laugh, and maybe fall a little in love. Spending time there always makes life feel like a smooth ride on a clean wave: painless, undemanding and very, very gro-oovy.

> *"Spending time there always makes life feel like*
> *a smooth ride on a clean wave: painless,*
> *undemanding and very, very gro-oovy."*

My first two years in Hawai'i mirrored a day at Sans Souci. I was traveling light and unencumbered, a solitary skiff skimming the surface of shallow water. Three, maybe four times a week, I'd finish class and scooter to the beach in ten minutes flat, unless I stopped for malasadas[1] along the way. When I returned to Hawai'i after Mother's death, however, the wind was definitely out of my sails. Coursework preoccupied me, true. But I was also exhausted, not so much from schoolwork or grief, but from recurring nightmares whose terrifying visions woke me up night after night.

I've always been a dreamer of vivid dreams, especially about the sea. This is not surprising. Dreams often reflect the worlds in which we live and mine has been a watery world of islands

---

[1] A delicious, sugary Portuguese-style doughnut that is best eaten when hot

and peninsulas, boats, bridges, ferries, rivers and bays. Even the patterns of my life resemble more the rolling swell of the sea rather than the flatness of the plains, the stillness of the desert or the high peaks and deep valleys of the mountains. Usually my sea dreams are pleasant—diving with dolphins or lazily floating on gentle waters—and I wake from them feeling calm, refreshed or even energized. But the currents of my sea dreams after Mother's death carried with them dark undertows that dragged me out to sea, or gigantic tidal waves that loomed over me as I struggled up the beach away from them. These briny nightmares continued without abating until it got so I dreaded falling asleep at night for fear of what I might see in my darkness.

One rainy Sunday morning, upset from another dream, I pulled on my slicker, fired up the moped and took off on a random ride through the city's neighborhoods of Manoa, Kaimuki, Palolo and Kahala. Rounding Diamond Head, instead of bearing right to return to the university, I turned toward Kapiolani Park and into the parking lot of Sans Souci. No one was there. It was too wet out. So I parked and walked through the drizzle to the water's edge where I plopped down like a soggy puddle before the vast Pacific Ocean. I was thankful that there was barely a wave in sight. I'd had enough of waves.

I sat in the tepid rain for a while mulling over my troubling sea dreams. Why was I having them? What did they symbolize? How could I stop them? I knew fear brought them on with greater frequency and intensity. Perhaps if I understood their meaning, I wouldn't dread them so much. And if I didn't dread them so much, maybe they would cease. Were they reflecting my secret worries and fears? How I felt about myself, my abilities or even my life? Could these dreams be my subconscious trying to wash away the emotional debris built up over the years? I'd taken Psych 101. I knew a bit about dream analysis. What I didn't know was how to make the dreams stop. And I needed them to stop because they were driving me crazy.

The rain grew from a drizzle to a downpour. Time to leave. As I stood, something in the water caught my eye; a vague, bubble-like shape bobbing in a cloud of debris near the jetty. Without considering, I waded toward it, clothes and all, until the water was nearly shoulder high. As I reached its sparkling wetness, I thought, could it be? Here? In Waikiki? A hollow green glass ball. A glass fishing float!

How did it manage to slip through the confines of a fishing net in some faraway sea and float thousands of miles through waves, winds and currents, past the crush of coral reefs, transpacific tankers and the monstrous mouths of baleen whales to arrive intact off the shores of Waikiki, Hawai'i? But here it was. A gift from the sea. To me.

I picked the float up and waded back to shore, considering: maybe I should be more like this fishing float. Instead of fearing my sea dreams, I should just let them wash over me, trusting that they will eventually lead me to a safe haven. Maybe, like the lovely fishing float, or the young child in Philip Booth's poem, *First Lesson*,[2] I should simply lie back and let the sea hold me. "Lie back, daughter," the father says, "...when you tire on the long thrash to your island... when fear cramps your heart ...lie gently and wide to the light-year stars, lie back, and the sea will hold you."

That night I placed the fishing float on my bedside table. A talisman, it became the last thing I saw at night and the first thing I saw in the morning. Each day, as I became less unsettled by my nightmares, their violence seemed to diminish until, one morning, I woke up from a dream of gentle waves cresting on a steady sea.

Though I always keep a lookout, I've never found another glass fishing float or, indeed, any other gift from the sea remotely like it. Perhaps it is because there are fewer of them to be found. Or perhaps it's because I've never needed to find one as much as I did back then.

---

[2] *First Lesson*, a poem about faith and conquering fear, was written by one of my favorite poets, New Englander Philip Booth (1925-2007).

> Lie back daughter, let your head
> be tipped back in the cup of my hand.
> Gently, and I will hold you. Spread
> your arms wide, lie out on the stream
> and look high at the gulls. A dead-
> man's float is face down. You will dive
> and swim soon enough where this tidewater
> ebbs to the sea. Daughter, believe
> me, when you tire on the long thrash
> to your island, lie up, and survive.
> As you float now, where I held you
> and let go, remember when fear
> cramps your heart what I told you:
> lie gently and wide to the light-year
> stars, lie back, and the sea will hold you.

The Consummate Beachcomber

Hawai'i and Waikiki

Hawai'i is the most isolated place on earth. There are about 18 commonly accepted islands in the Hawaiian *archipelago*[1] including eight main islands: O'ahu, Maui, Hawai'i (aka, the *Big Island*), Moloka'i, Lana'i, Kaua'i, Ni'ihau and Kaho'olawe.[2] These islands are the visible remains of ancient giant undersea volcanoes. Some islands are made up of at least one primary volcano although others, like the Big Island,[3] are composites of two or more volcanoes (some still active). Hawai'i boasts extensive exotic flora and some of the best surfing beaches in the world.

Archaeologists believe the islands were first settled between 300 and 700 CE with the arrival of Polynesian voyagers from the Marquesas Islands. Over the centuries, a highly stratified culture evolved with a formidable kapu system ensuring that scarce island resources not be depleted. In 1627 Spanish sailors visited Hawai'i and, in a ship's log, described seeing a volcanic eruption. By the time Captain James Cook arrived in 1778, hundreds of thousands of Hawaiians resided in the islands. Later, in 1779, the archipelago became famous when Captain Cook was killed at Kealakekua Bay on the Big Island during a dispute with Hawaiians. Shortly thereafter, Hawai'i entered a period of civil wars (1782) between rival chiefs that finally ended in 1810 when Chief Kamehameha unified the islands into one kingdom.

Over the next 90 years Hawai'i underwent a number of significant changes: the 1820 arrival of Protestant missionaries from New England (who came to "do good" and did very well indeed); the introduction of cash crops such as pineapple and sugar; and waves of immigrants from Japan, Portugal, China, Puerto Rico, Okinawa, Korea and the Philippines. It also weathered a series of political power plays by the Russians, English, French and, particularly, the Americans. In 1895 the U.S. forced Hawaiian Queen Lili'uokalani to abdicate her throne and three years later annexed Hawai'i as a U.S. territory.

In 1935, despite the introduction of air service by Pan Am between Hawai'i and the mainland (a flight that took 22 hours!), Hawai'i remained a sleepy, romantic hideaway of pineapple and sugar plantations, surfers and canoe paddlers. But after the Japanese bombed Pearl Harbor in 1941, the world took notice. The islands soon became overrun with soldiers and U.S. government personnel, many of whom returned to live there after the war ended. The islands also became popular as a getaway spot for Hollywood celebrities because of the anonymity they enjoyed there. After statehood in 1959, the general public gradually warmed to Hawai'i as an exotic place to holiday. By the 1970s, tourism was a leading source of revenue for the state.

---

[1] An *archipelago* is group of scattered islands. If one includes the 100-plus islets spread out in the Hawaiian chain, the state comprises about 120 islands.

[2] The other 10 islands include Ka'ula, a small island situated near Ni'ihau, and nine land masses north of Kaua'i, called the Northwest Hawaiian Islands.

[3] The Big Island is comprised of five volcanoes including the world's largest active volcano, Mauna Loa, as well its most productive one, Kilauea.

A float with friends: a baleen whale tooth, a barnacle-studded rock, and a Japanese carved fish

"How did it manage to...float thousands of miles through waves,
winds and currents, past the crush of coral reefs, transpacific tankers
and the monstrous mouths of baleen whales to arrive intact off the shores of
Waikiki, Hawai'i? But here it was. A gift from the sea. To me."

To many people, Waikiki represents *the* vision of tropic romance, with its long sweep of sandy beach framed by Diamond Head crater, its palm trees, tiki torches and ukulele-playing beach boys. Visitors as far back as Mark Twain and Robert Louis Stevenson enjoyed its beauty and leisurely pace. Today, warm water temperatures year-round, balmy breezes, waves gentle enough for novice surfers and proximity to beautiful Kapiolani Park and Honolulu, make Waikiki an ideal place to spend a pleasant day.

"Hawai'i remained a sleepy,
romantic hideaway of pineapple and sugar plantations,
surfers and canoe paddlers."

Glass Fishing Floats

Throughout the world, glass fishing floats (*sea bubbles*) are a favorite beachcombing treasure. First designed in 1844 by Christopher Faye, a Norwegian, the hollow glass balls were introduced as a means to make Norway's cod fishing industry more efficient in the frigid Arctic, North Sea and North Atlantic waters. Woven into the rope line of fishing nets, the floats make the nets more buoyant. Inevitably, however, rough currents, high waves and storms rip many floats loose, sometimes scattering them thousands of miles from their point of origin. Miraculously, many floats, some with fish netting still attached, wash ashore intact. By the 1930s glass fishing floats could be found all over the world as other fishermen, especially Japanese, Korean and Chinese who fished throughout the Pacific Ocean region, enthusiastically adopted the technology.

Authentic glass floats are usually made of hand-blown heavy glass with a seal button (or *blob button*) placed over the hole when the blowpipe is removed. Usually a bubble, or *nubbin*, is inside the seal button and smaller air bubbles are scattered throughout the float. Fishing floats come in different shapes, including round and rolling pin, and range in size from 5 to 18 inches. Norwegian floats, which are a dark glass stamped with IV or V, are in great demand by collectors. The pretty, more common Asian floats are usually found in beachy colors of sea foam, light green or light blue-green though beachcombers have also found floats colored olive green, aqua, amber, teal, pink and gray.

Many fishing floats are frosted from the sand and salty surf. Frosting occurs when a float is beached on coarse gravel or sand and then rolled around in the surf. If a float has no sign of wear, it was probably never actually used and, in fact, may have been produced solely for the tourist market. As fishing fleets switch from glass floats to Styrofoam and plastic ones, it is becoming increasingly difficult to find glass floats while beachcombing. The best places to look for them are on remote ocean beaches. Shards of broken floats strewn along rocky coastlines, on the other hand, are still relatively easy to find. Much of this glass, however, lacks the frosted weathering that comes from being buffed by the sand.

Chapter 19
Ocean Stars

Let go and let fate decide.

A beautiful tapestry turban shell from Tonga nesting in a clam shell bed of miniature sea urchins and sea biscuits from the Caribbean

'Emeline Beach, Tonga: *Ocean Stars*

Let go and let fate decide.

Beachcombing is a journey, not a competitive sport. Finding special treasures really has little to do with skill or ability or even with being the first on the beach. Sure, timing, location and experience can weigh the odds in our favor, but that only works up to a point. Too many other factors totally out of our control come into play (the moon, wind and tides), which can lift and lower sea levels or power waves to shore. This, in turn, can wash up new treasures mere seconds after we've moved on. So the race to "get there first" doesn't always matter in beachcombing.

What matters more is the ability to let go and be present. Because we have so little say about what shows up on the shore on any given day, beachcombing forces us to suspend our all-too-human tendencies to always try to manipulate events and orchestrate outcomes. Instead, we learn to simply let the search lead where it may. Some days it might not lead to much, but seasoned beachcombers know how to make the best of situations not of their own design. If there are no shells one day, maybe there will be sea urchins or interesting pieces of coral. Or maybe not. *Que sera, sera.* What will be, will be. And if it's a day of slim pickings, the body still benefits from the fresh air and exercise, and the mind and spirit, granted temporary reprieve from the strain of driving one's destiny, are uplifted.

Then, when least expected, magic happens; a worn red marble tumbles in on a wave, or a shard of china etched with medieval castles pokes out from a clump of seaweed. Beach explorers are thrilled by such moments of random discovery much the same way children are at the first sight of presents under a Christmas tree.

The beachcomber's lesson of "letting go and letting fate" hit home the year I returned to Tonga for doctoral field research. I was an unmarried thirty-something and, though I'd dated some wonderful men over the years, I'd never seriously considered marriage, preferring instead to move in time to the rhythm of my own whims and moods. But after Mother's death an uncomfortable, untethered feeling took hold, as if I'd been set adrift in unfamiliar territory with no map to guide me or roots to hold me down. If I disappeared tomorrow, no one would notice for days, maybe even weeks; a revelation I found more depressing than emancipating. The idea of a husband, children, lumpy sofas and crayon drawings on the fridge suddenly became appealing.

Finally, I reach a point in my life where I'm ready to settle down and what was I doing? Moving back to Tonga, where all the men my age were either already married or not marriage material. But what would it matter anyway? By Tongan standards I was already "over the hill."

My first month back in the Kingdom—when I wasn't conducting research—was spent making a cursory review of dating "possibilities." Always, the men came up short: too wild, too crazy, too dull, too traditional, too dumb, too married, too married, too married. I'd take my frustrations down to the beach for long strolls, lingering until the blue hour—*l'heure bleu* the French call it—my favorite time of day. That time between twilight and dusk when clarity and mystery meet and mingle before darkness closes in and strings the sky with stars. Equatorial stars; so close to earth you can almost touch them.

One constellation in that celestial ceiling always caught my eye. It was Pleiades, named for the seven Greek sisters Zeus transformed into doves (*pleiades*) to shield them from the relentless ardor of the hunter Orion. Tongans refer to the constellation as *Mataliki*, or "little eyes," because their seafaring ancestors depended on it to guide them safely across the immense Pacific Ocean. About the only place Pleiades guided me was along a tired city beach. But it was a curious constellation. Fun. A tease. For whenever I turned my full gaze upon it, the stars dissipated into a vague, boring blur of light. But if I turned away slightly and looked at it out of the corner of my eye, each star burst forth with stunning clarity and the constellation transformed into a twinkling cluster of ladies dancing in the night sky.

Sometimes on my walks I played hide-and-seek with Pleiades, shifting my gaze back and forth to make the stars recede, pop out, recede, pop out. I came to think of these sister stars as galactic messengers trying to alert me to some important truth cogent to my current situation. Something like, "Don't be like Orion, always trying to force the future. If he hadn't pushed so hard and scared us all off, he'd be married by now with hundreds of kids. So lighten up. Concentrate on the tasks at hand. Let your life unfold as it will."

Heeding this "heavenly advice," I decided to turn my attention to what I could control (my research activities) and stop worrying about what I couldn't control (my love life, or lack thereof). If I kept occupied meeting with farmers, tromping around their muddy plantations by day and taking notes around kerosene lanterns in their huts by night, my future would hopefully take care of itself. And that's just what happened. Over the next few months my attention became so diverted by these activities that I stopped worrying, or even caring, about my future. In fact, I no longer wanted a serious relationship. I was too busy. And the timing was wrong. I'd be returning to Hawai'i in five months. I had too much work to do and needed to focus on my research.

And wouldn't you know? That's exactly when fate decided to step in, washing my future up to me in much the same way a wave washes treasures up just moments after you've abandoned the search. The moment I stopped focusing on Pleiades, the stars appeared before my eyes. The moment I stopped caring about my future, it strolled into my life with a handsome bearing, a swinging gait and a bemused expression; nothing like what I'd envisioned but everything for which I'd hoped.

Four months after meeting, we married and spent our honeymoon picnicking on different beaches across Tongatapu, each picnic a simple, uncluttered affair of easy meals, long swims and longer naps. Usually, after a dip and some lunch, we pulled our towels under a tree and snoozed to the sound of waves breaking and palm fronds clacking in the breeze. When I couldn't sleep, I beachcombed or else just lay, staring out to sea, my head resting on my sleeping husband's tummy. This is what contentment is, I thought. There is no place else I'd rather be, nothing else I'd rather do and no one else I'd rather be with. And I thanked my lucky stars.

Our favorite beach was 'Emeline, far away from villages and tourist haunts. On 'Emeline it was just us, some flying terns and an occasional school of dolphins. One afternoon there, as my husband slept, I lay beside him lazily studying some fine grains of sand attached to my hand. I realized that, like Pleiades, if I stared too intently at them, their colors blurred into a sea of beige. But when I relaxed the intensity of my gaze, lovely specks of color burst forth in lively shades of pink and lavender and green. Confetti colors. Like a party.

As I scooped up more sand to examine, a small green shell tumbled out. A snail shell with baby barnacles attached to its pointy top and intricate, swirling designs of sea green, azure and white across its body. The patterns on the shell resembled clouds and rivers and valleys and I was reminded of those photos of planet Earth taken from outer space. "They have brought me a snail," e.e. cummings writes. "Inside it sings a map-green ocean. My heart swells with water …" My shell did look like a map of the world. A world I was familiar with. A world called love.

Nowadays, in the hectic hours of family life, I depend on my pretty 'elili (turban) shell to remind me of those slow afternoons of honeymoon picnics when it was just the two of us.

And I thank my lucky stars for the lesson that beachcombing with Pleiades[1] taught me: that sometimes, the best way to travel in life is to just to get out of destiny's way.

[1] The Japanese call Pleiades *subaru* which means "united" or "getting together." Japanese farmers, on the other hand, named the constellation *suharu*, for "seeds" because, to them, the stars resemble seed bundles and, when the constellation rises in the sky, it reminds them to plant their crops. After nearly 25 years of marriage, I'd say Pleiades stayed true to all her definitions in Greek, Tongan, Japanese and the language of love.

The Consummate Beachcomber

More on Tonga

Tonga is composed of a chain of islands formed along the tops of two parallel submarine ridges. Strung 277 miles from north to south, they range from peaked volcanic islands (some with rain forests) to the proverbial sandy tropical islands to teeny, rocky islet "buds" that periodically pop up, then disappear below sea level again. These "Jack-in-the-Box" islands are caused by small, periodic underwater volcanic eruptions that spew up loose volcanic material that is soon washed away by the sea.

The western ridge of the island group displays many high volcanoes, both active and inactive, while the eastern ridge is composed of scattered, low-lying coral islands. Some of the volcanic islands such as Kao, Late, Tafahi and Fonualei are dormant while two others, Tofua and Niuafo'ou, have had such violent eruptions that their cones have blown off. (The huge calderas left behind are now lakes.) The volcano on Niuafo'ou, in particular, has been very active over the last century, erupting nine times. Its most recent eruption in 1946 was so violent that all 1,300 inhabitants had to be evacuated. (Many have since returned despite the probability of another eruption at any time.) The mantle of volcanic ash resulting from these eruptions are the source of the rich, fertile soils which contribute to the Kingdom's reputation as a leading producer of agricultural commodities in the region.

The eastern ridge of Tonga's island chain is markedly different from the western chain for it is comprised of small, coral islands that have been built up over millions of years by colonies of *coral polyps* (tiny marine animals). As the polyps grow, they extract salt from the water and build it into outer skeletons of very hard limestone that, over time, evolve into islands. Eventually, huge reef systems form around the limestone islands, providing excellent habitat for exotic mollusks and fish species. The fine white beach sand on these islands is composed of a combination of calcium carbonate and limestone from the breakdown of shells and limestone reef.

Tapestry Turban Shells

Turban shells, a univalve gastropod from the Turbinidae family, are found around coral reefs throughout the tropical waters of the Indo-Pacific region. Colors, textures and designs vary greatly in this shell family. Tapestry turbans are thick, heavy and glossy. Some come with intricate ornamental patterning and a variety of colors, the most common being a dark reddish brown with darker bands dotted, blotched and striped with a creamy white. All tapestry turbans have an *operculum*, or trap door, which is a rounded piece of hard shell attached to the gastropod's foot. The blueish-green and brown color of this operculum, popularly referred to as a *cat's eye*, is often incorporated into jewelry.

Afterword

The Sand's Shifting Contours

Life is about taking chances.
Nothing ventured, nothing gained.

An antique porcelain campaign button
from the early 1900s surrounded by rocks
and chunks of old brick

153

Any Beach, Anywhere: *The Sand's Shifting Contours*

Life is about taking chances. Nothing ventured, nothing gained.

Eighty-mile-per-hour winds last night. Lightning. Tornado warnings. The tide so high, the jetties were totally submerged by waves. I sent my eldest son down to drag the Adirondack chairs up to the road, fearing they'd be swept out to sea. This morning, stranded on the berm, they appear lost and confused. And the morning beach, hammered by last night's waves, is flattened like a dog's ears when it's being punished. Catamarans upended. Picnic tables half-buried. No animal tracks crisscross the shoreline. Only a few bold stones lift their noses from the sand, as if sniffing the air to see if it's safe to emerge.

This is the third bad storm in as many months and the beach has sorely suffered. Storms, overbuilding and the seawater rise from global warming have left precious little sand on our shores. Nor are the contours of the beach as smooth or welcoming. Instead, they are sharp, irregular and, in some places, jagged; the top layer of sand blown away to expose an oily, silty clay beneath. Sturdy stuff. Hard to penetrate. But not as sweet to the touch as fine-grained sand. Crusty patches of iron ore are also exposed. Finally, a geologic explanation for all the flat ore fragments we use in rock-skipping contests.

I can relate to the way the beach looks today: embattled, worn, spent. I feel that way, too. In an effort to calm myself, I try breathing deeply and slowly as I walk. I stare at the apricot sunlight streaking through the clouds and across a periwinkle sky. I try to feel happy about the piece of dark green beach glass I find and pocket. (Maybe it's from a 200-year-old Dutch onion-shaped bottle?) But when intrusive, defeatist thinking bangs on the psyche's door, it's hard work to keep one's mood elevated. Today's thinking goes something like: this mid-life crisis of wanting to resume a writing career has only gotten us deeper in debt. What was I thinking…? Who am I to…? Really, I'm such a failure. (A broke failure at that.) Then the tears come. In public, too. How pathetic. Blubbering like a whale in a strong wind and not a tissue in sight.

I know I'm just suffering from a bout of self doubt compounded by high blood pressure. Nothing new. Otherwise, I'm in good health and it's a spectacularly clear, if cold, autumn day. Where's the old fighting spirit? The give-it-your-best-shot attitude? This is just a lull; the niggling little "no, No, NO!" toddler voice craving attention.

"Don't give in to 'no' voices," Mother used to say. "You're made of sterner stuff! So straighten up and stay on track."

Okay! Okay! I turn for home and walk down a few more beaches. As I pass by clumps of matted dune grass, limp from last night's siege, I spot an oval-shaped object amongst them. I lift it up and see it's a porcelain pin with a broken clasp. Could be a century old. I turn it over and read the words "Lawrence for Governor." A campaign button? Now that's weird. Where'd it come from? Who was Lawrence? And did he win? The button on the beach is yet another of life's many mysteries to explore.

Nearing home, I meet a neighbor walking her dog. I like this neighbor very much. She's a gracious person, always friendly and upbeat. She is also fighting for her life against a cancer that insists on returning.[1] Her hair is gone but not her hopefulness. We chat briefly and I show her the button. She responds with interest, then, smiling, waves so long and we go our separate ways.

What was I thinking feeling so sorry for myself? My neighbor has not lost her spunk and she is in a battle for her life. Old Lawrence ran for Governor and, even if he lost, he tried. Everyone doubts themselves sometimes and sure, some ventures fail. But there is glory in the effort of following your dream, of moving ahead despite the odds to see if you can make something happen that is important to you. True, taking a professional gamble in mid-life, particularly if children are still at home and money is tight, is not for the faint-hearted or weak-kneed. And when the willies come, sometimes all you can do is shake them off, stay the course and keep taking that leap of faith; the one that promises everything will turn out right (even if it sometimes won't). Because what is the alternative? For me, it was a life of dreams buried under mounds of dirty clothes and breakfast dishes, and ambitions derailed by exploitative bosses who took pleasure in humiliating their underpaid employees.

So, I will say "Yes" to the challenge. Like a beach in a storm, I may feel overwhelmed or a bit battered but come the dawn, I'll rise like a phoenix and get on with the writing, doubts be damned.

To those of you reading this book right now, many thanks for supporting my dream. Now it's time for me to move on to other books and other beaches. And you? My hope is that, when you close this book, you'll take your own stroll on a beach. Time is short and treasures await. Storms do, too. But remember, it is storms that reveal the many treasures hidden in the sand.

[1] Thankfully, she is in remission and enjoys many walks on the beach.

Bibliography

GENERAL BIBLIOGRAPHY

http://www.beachcombersalert.org, http://www.drbeachcomb.com, http://www.enature.com, http://www.infoplease.com, http://www.lonely planet.com, http://www.nature.org, http://www.noaa.gov, http://www.njscuba.net , http://www.oceaninn. com, http://www.open2.net/coast/ancestorscoast.html, http://sherpaguides.com, http://www.seed.slb.com, http://www.wisegeek.com, http://www.vims.edu

Berrill, N.J. and Jaquelyn, *1001 Questions Answered About the Seashore*, Dover Publications, Inc., N. Y., 1957
Fagan, Brian M., *Ancient North America*, Thames and Hudson, McCash, London, 1981
Groushko, Mike, *Treasure: Lost, Found, and Undiscovered*, Courage Books, Philadelphia, PA, 1990
Kavanaugh, James, *Pocket Naturalist: Animal Tracks*, Waterford Press, China, 2000
Robbins, Sarah Fraser and Yentsch, Clarice, *The Sea is all About Us*, Harcourt Brace Jovanovich, Inc. 1973
Trefil, James S., *A Scientist at the Shore*, Collier Books, MacMillan Publishing Co., N.Y., 1984

BEACH TREASURES
Ceramics:
McHale, Jean, "Tips for Buying Antiques," Chesapeake Home Magazine, October-November 2005, pgs. 112-122
Patterson, Jerry E., *Porcelain*, prepared by the Cooper-Hewitt Museum, The Smithsonian Illustrated Library of Antiques, Smithsonian Institution, Washington, D.C., 1979

Doorknobs:
http://www.antiquedoorknobs.org, http://www.bronzebells.com/whybronze.html

Fishing Floats:
http://www.beachcombersalert.org/JapaneseGlassBalls.html, http://home.comcast.net/~4miller/home.html

Farnsworth, Stu and Alan D. Rammer, *Glass Fishing Floats*, Farnsworth and Rammer Publishing, Oregon, 2005
Pich, Walt, *Glass Ball; A Comprehensive Guide for Oriental Glass Fishing Floats Founds on Pacific Beaches*, Walter C. Pich Publishing, 2004

Rocks:
http://www.minerals.net, http://www.smenet.org

Carruthers, Margaret and Iselin, Josie, *Beach Stones*, Harry N. Abrahms, Inc., 2006
Oldale, Robert N., "Cape Cod's 'Magic' Quartz Pebbles," The Cape Naturalist, 1997, pp 44-45

Sea Glass, Bottles, and Fishing Floats:
http://www.bottlebooks.com , http://www.geocities.com/balbottles/index.html, http://www.seaglassassociation.com, http://home.comcast.net/~4miller/aboutfloats/about.html

Ketchum, William C., Jr., *A Treasury of American Bottles*, A Rutledge Book, Bobbs-Merrill, N.Y. 1975
LaMotte, Richard, *Pure Sea Glass*, Chesapeake Sea Glass Publishing, Chestertown, MD, 2004

Shells:
http://www.beach-net.com/Oceanshellslist.html, http://www.beachcomberscompanion.net, http://www.conchologistsofamerica.org, http://www.enature.com, http://www.mitchellspublications.com/guides/shells/, http://www.reefed.edu.au, http://www.seashells.org, http://www.seashellworld.com, http://www.seashell-collector.com

Cassie, Brian, *National Audubon Society First Field Guide: Shells*, Scholastic Inc., N. Y., 2000
Dance, S. Peter, *Shells*, A Dorling Kindersley Handbook, N.Y., 1992
Douglass, Jackie Leatherbury and John, Peterson *First Guides: Shells*, Houghton Mifflin Company, 1989
Eisenberg, Jerome M., *A Collector's Guide to Seashells of the World*, McGraw-Hill Book Company, N.Y., 1981

ATLANTIC OCEAN and CARIBBEAN REGION

http://www.cape-ann.com/history, http://www.marthas-vineyard.com , http://www.coastalga.com, http://www.delawarehistory.gov, http://www.delawareliving.com/history, http://www.floridacommunitystudies.org, http://www.floridastateparks.org, http://www.gloucesterma.com, http://www.history.com, http://www.history.vineyard.net, http://www.indianz.com, http://www.ja-maicans.com, http://www.jekyllisland.com, http://www.key-biscayne.com, http://www.mvol.com/directory/government/#2289, http://www.nantucket.beach.net, http://www.nantucketchamber.org, http://www.n-georgia.com, http://www.oceangrovehistory.org, http://www.pequothotel.com, http://www.pilgrims.net , http://www.query.nytimes.com, http://www.russpickett.com/history, http://www.sanibel-captiva.org, http://www.swagga.com/rasta.htm, http://www.trashskimmer.com/pp.srbc.htm, http://www.woodshole.er.usgs.gov

Brandon, William, *Indians*, American Heritage Publishing Co., 1975
Hall, June, *Jekyll Island's Early Years: From Prehistory Through Reconstruction*, Wormsloe Foundation Publications, University of Georgia Press 2005
Morris, Allen, *Florida Name Places*, Pineapple Press, Inc., Miami 1995
Oldale, Robert N., *Cape Cod, Martha's Vineyard and Nantucket: The Geologic Story*, Cape Cod Publications, Yarmouth Port, MA, 2001

CHESAPEAKE BAY REGION

http://www.baydreaming.com, http://www.bayridge.org, http://www.cbf.org, http://www.chesapeakebay.net, http://dnr.state.md.us, http://www.hometownannapolis.com, http://www.mcdaniel.edu, http://www.mdarchives.state.med, http://www.mgs.md.gov/esic/fs/fs6, http://www.mrsouthcounty.com

"Antiques in Annapolis," reprinted from The Magazine, Antiques, by Historic Annapolis, Inc., Annapolis, MD. 1977
Ashby, Wallace L., *Fossils of Calvert Cliffs*, Calvert Marine Museum, Solomons, MD, 1979
Burns, Jasper, *Fossil Collecting in the Mid-Atlantic States*, The Johns' Hopkins University Press, Baltimore, MD, 1991
Davis, Derring, *Annapolis Houses*, Bonanza Books, NY, 1947
Patterson, Carol and McWilliams, Jane, *Bay Ridge on the Chesapeake*, Brighton Editions, MD, 1986
Poag, Wylie C., *Chesapeake Invader*, Princeton University Press, Princeton, NJ, 1999

NORTH SEA: ORKNEY ISLANDS and SHETLAND ISLANDS

http://www.bbc.co.uk/history/scottishhistory, http://www.fettes.com/shetland., http://www.genuki.org.uk, http://www.goldmineland.co.uk/history.html, http://www.historic-uk.com/HistoryUK/Scotland-Histor, http://www.iknow-scotland.co.uk, http://www.mosiac.lk.net/timeline.html, http://www.scandinavica.com/shet-ork.htm, http://www.shetlandhamefarin.com, http://www.undiscoveredscotland.co.uk, http://unst.org, http://www.visitorkney.com

Welcome to the Orkney Islands, Orkney Tourist Organization, William MacDonald, Ltd., Edinburgh, 1978
Ritchie, Anna and Graham, *The Ancient Monuments of Orkney*, Her Majesty's Stationary Office, Edinburgh, 1978

PACIFIC OCEAN and SOUTH PACIFIC REGION

http://www.amsamoa.net, http://www.i-beaches.info/california/stinson.htm, http://www.britishmuseum.org, http://www.hawaii-nation.com, http://www.lava.net/~poda/history.html, http://www.planet-tonga.com, http://pubs.usgs.gov/circ/c1198/chapters/162-176_MarineMammals , http://www.samoanet.com/amsamoa, http://www.soest.hawaii.edu/GG/hcv.html, http://www.stinsonbeachonline.com

Bellwood, Peter, *The Polynesians*, Thames and Hudson, London, 1978
Campbell, I. C., *Island Kingdom: Tonga Ancient and Modern*, Canterbury University Press, 1992
Crane, E.A., *The Geography of Tonga*, Crane Publishing, Government Printing Office, Nuku'alofa, Tonga, 1979
Nordyke, Eleanor, C., *The Peopling of Hawaii*, U. of Hawaii Press, Honolulu 1989
Oliver, Douglaas, L., *The Pacific Islands*, U. of Hawaii Press, Hoinolulu, 1977
Ritterbush, S. Deacon, *Sometimes the Native Knows Best: A Discourse on Contextualization, Commercial Farming and Sustainable Development in the Kingdom of Tonga*, Ph.D. Dissertation, University of Hawaii, Honolulu 1994
Rutherford, Noel, *Friendly Islands*, Oxford University Press, Melbourne, 1977

Acknowledgements

Making a miracle happen takes Divine Providence, a (sometimes nervous) disregard for failure, a lot of hard work and a lot of help. I was fortunate to have a sufficient supply of all four ingredients to see this project through.

For those who travelled with me through the first leg of my life's journey, thanks for making the experience an interesting, enlightening and, in some cases, a more bearable one. I don't know where some of you are now but you will always be tucked into a corner of my heart: Lenora Ruggerio, Sharon Tastet, Reesa Motley, Thayer Larrimore, Michael Owen, Debbie Steed, Reid Hosford, Diane Moore, David Cronin, Lynn Graybeal, William Daffer, Lou Carter and Robin Beasley (Annapolis); Andy Leahy (New Jersey); Ann Parry, Curt Humphries, Dave Osmund and Debbie Clarke (Nantucket); Becca Scanlon and Lisa Young (American Samoa); Eddie Carlson, Isabella Maka, Kerry Brady, Fekitamoeloa 'Utoikamanu, Sieni Havea, the Vite family of Tokomololo and the Patolo family of Tafahi (Tonga); Kris and Dan Doherty, Mary and Justin Doebele, Jeffrey Mays, Philo Stefanides, Trudy Trumpy and Scott Chambers (Boston); Kitty Cook, Kathy Spaar and Lina Adrissi (D.C.); and Diana Shepard, Kanalei Shun, Ray Zeason, Pete Milone, Sohail Inayatullah, Paini Harris, Glennis Shearer and Barbara Schwaiger (Hawaii).

Thanks very much to those who shared their area expertise and/or memories with me: Jane McWilliams, Carole Patterson and Matt Grubbs (Maryland); Andy Leahy (New Jersey); Liz Golden (Florida); Betsy Upton (Jamaica); Julie Allinson and Beth Green (Nantucket); Lisa Young (Samoa); Tomasi Patolo and Ian Campbell (Tonga); Beth Gott and Nena Todd (Delaware); Robert Hurry (Calvert Cliffs); Robert Oldale and Margaret Carruthers (geology); and Richard LaMotte (sea glass and self-publishing). Many thanks also to Sydney Petty, Joan Carroll, Julie Allinson, Anne Owen, Trish Milone and Sandy Chun for assisting me with editing. The text benefited greatly from their suggestions. To my former cheerleading buddy and current partner-in-crime, Debbie Steed Russell, your good humor and talented editing skills were blessings. To my former waitressing pal and now very accomplished photographer, Celia Pearson, many thanks for your steadfast encouragement, the beautiful intro photo, and the introduction to fellow beachcomber and mentor, Richard LaMotte. To my talented and good-natured neighbors, Mac-wiz Tom Dunbar and graphic designer extraordinaire Jill Madsen, there's a night at the Ebb Tide on me after this! And special thanks always to dear and generous family and friends for their advice and for keeping my spirits buoyed, but especially to Charlie and Elinor Woodman, Shannon Brownlee, Po Martin, Manelle Martino, Sandy Sweeney, Alpine Byrd, Mary Lou Howe and Marilyn McGilvery. Thanks also to Sam Brown, and Drs. Lou Berman, Richard Katz and Angela Peterman (and you too, Eileen) for keeping us on the "family plan" during this period of belt tightening.

All those years casually chatting up strangers finally paid off when I met and joined forces with Megan Lloyd, an extremely gifted young photographer who proved so adept at transferring my creative visions to photo and book form. This has been quite a journey we've taken together, Megan, and I know your talents will take you far in the future.

Finally, I am blessed with a wonderful family who have forgone many pleasures over the last few years so that I could reawaken my dream of a writing career. I am indebted to you all. Kilino, Najeda, Severn and Tali, along with the beach, you are my first loves.